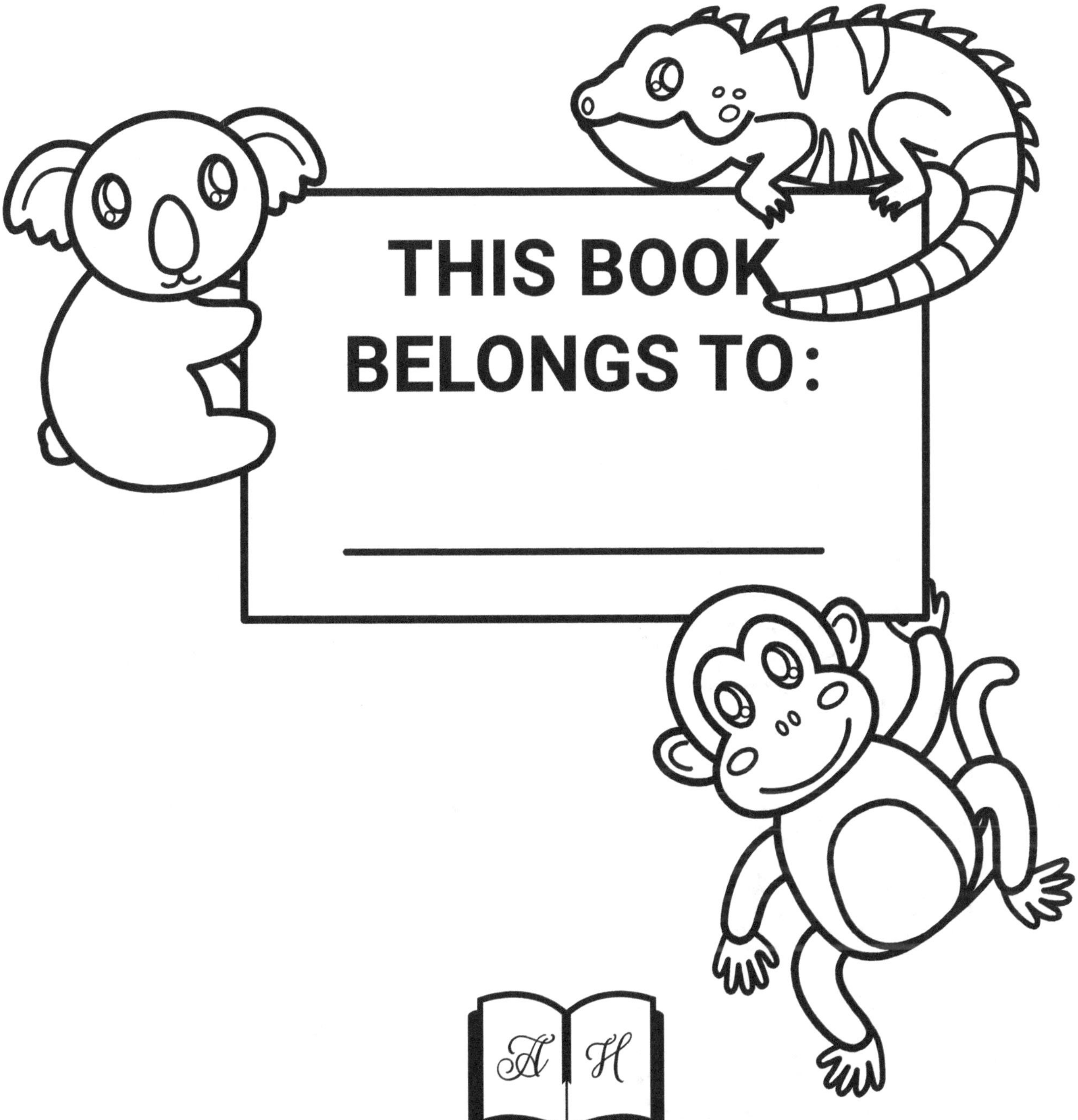

# THIS BOOK BELONGS TO:

________________

**ANGELA HAWKINS BOOK**



Please leave a review because we would like to know your thoughts, feedbacks and opinions to create better paperback products for you to enjoy!

Thank you for your support.

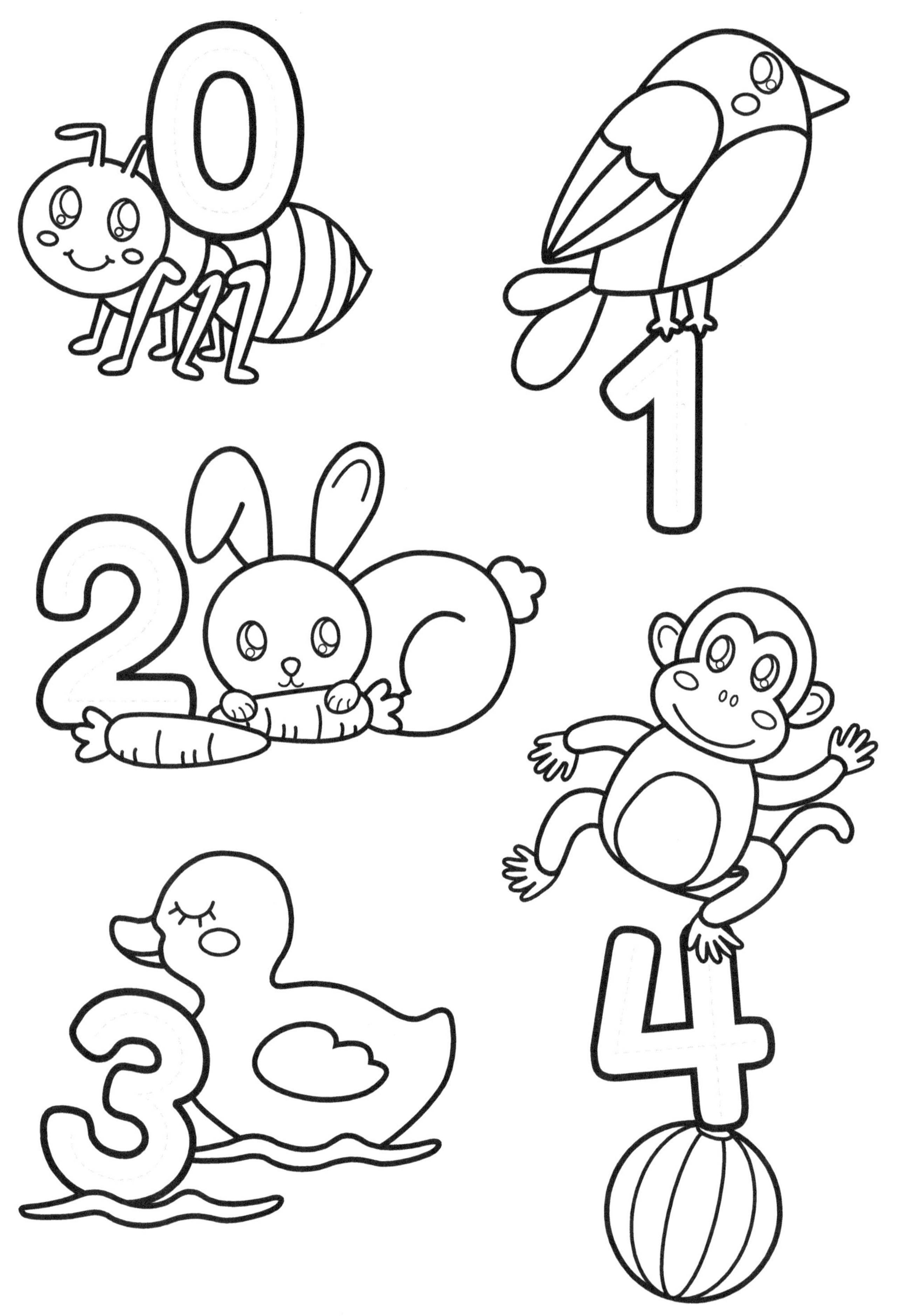

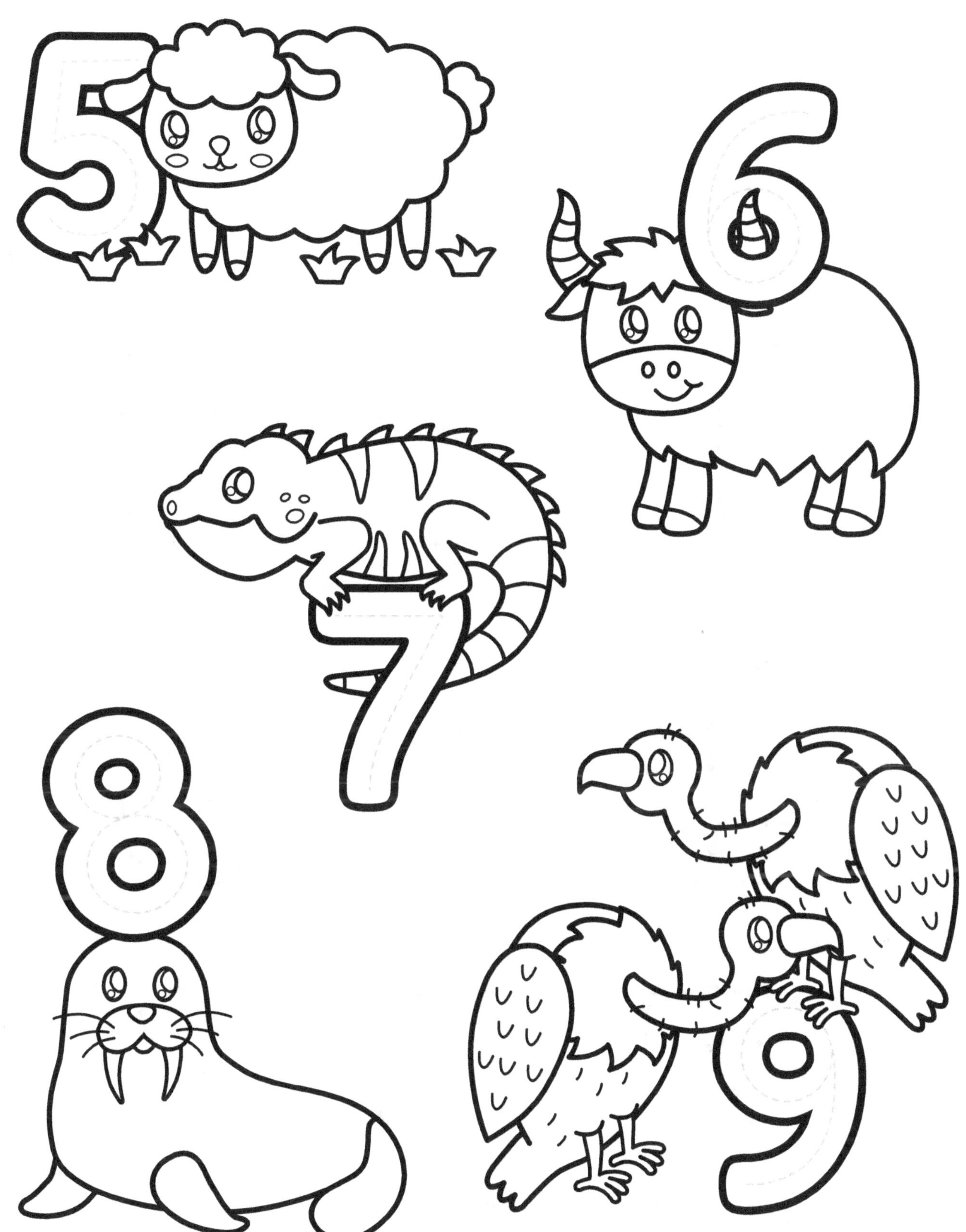

0

1 2 3

4 5 6

7 8 9

A B C D E
F G H I J K
L M N O P
Q R S T U
V W X Y Z

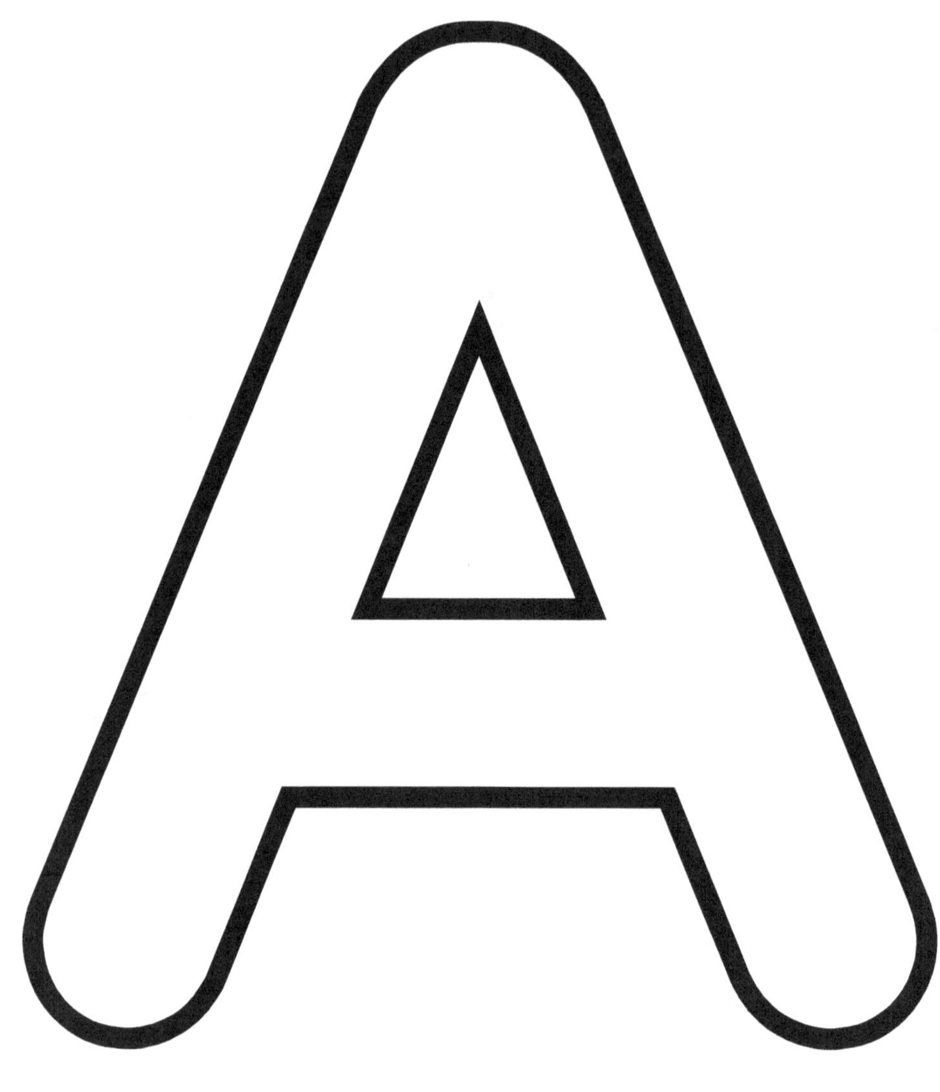

ANT

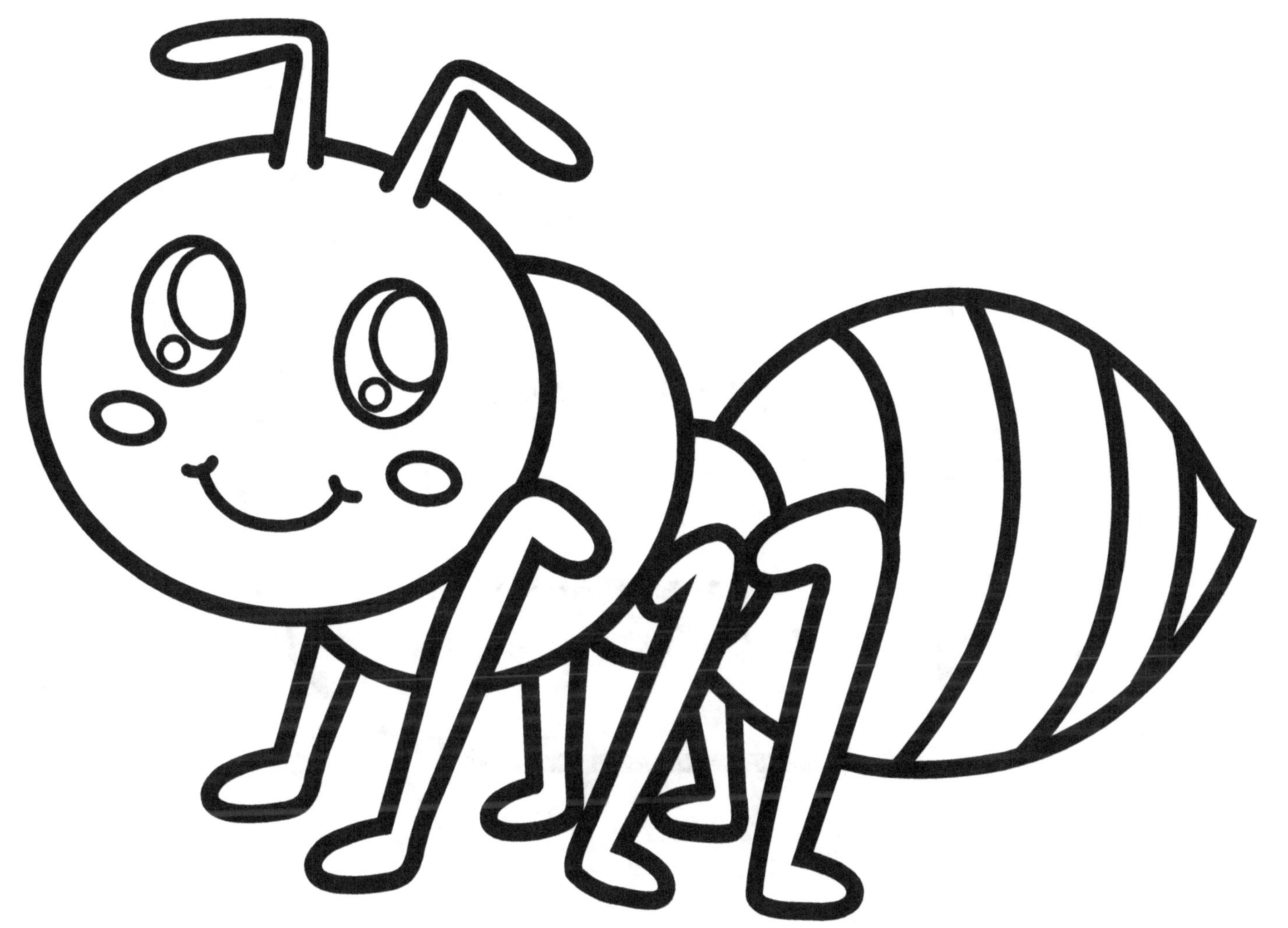

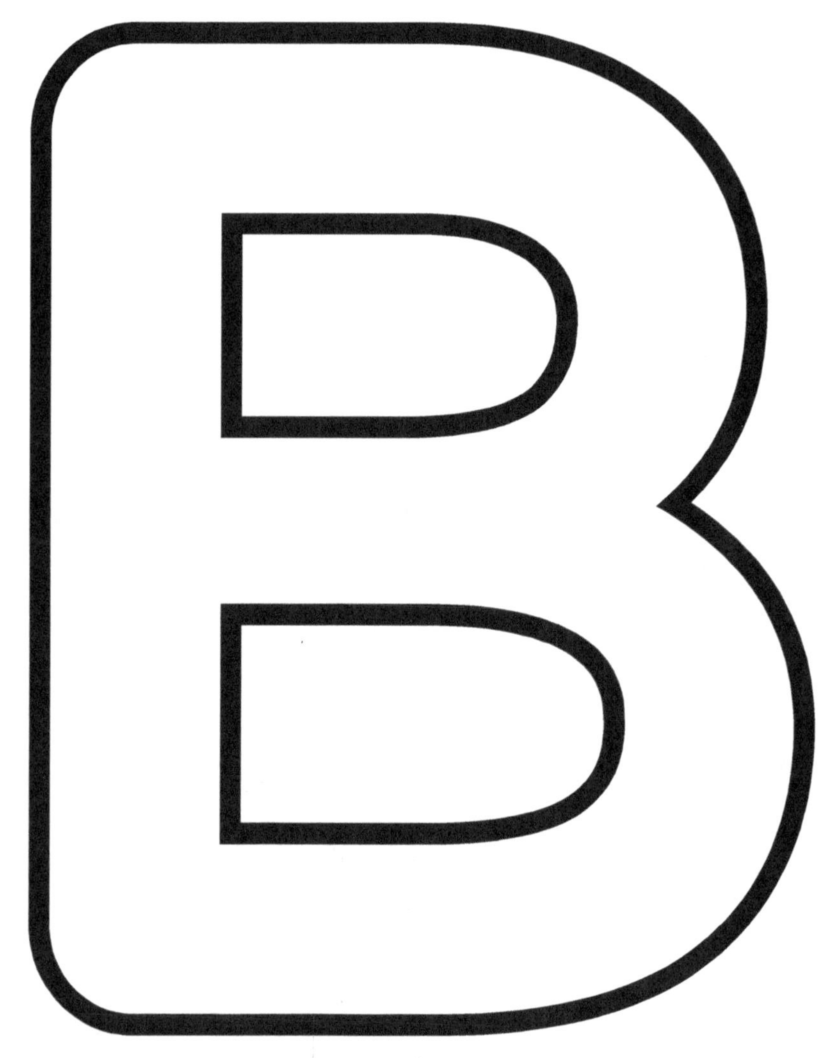

# BIRD

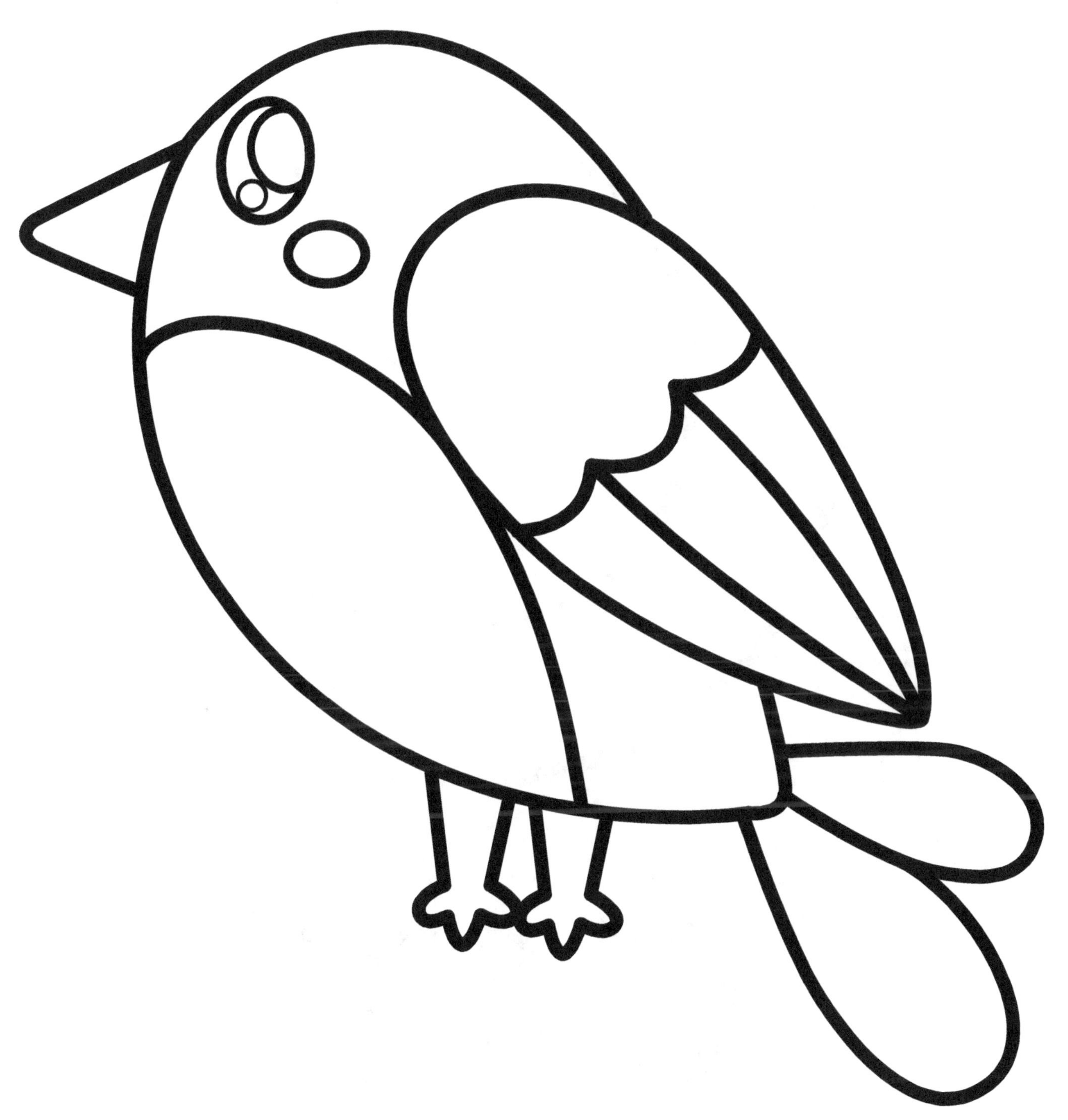

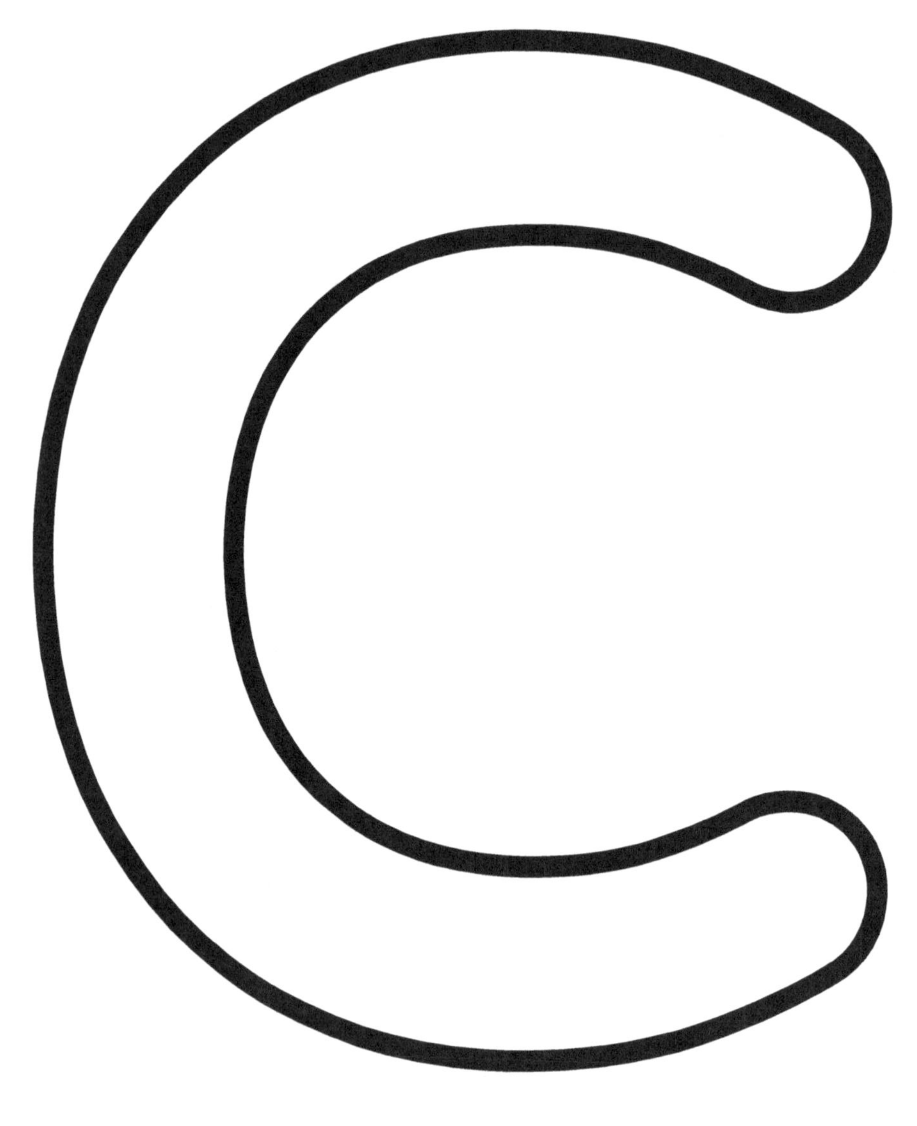

CAT

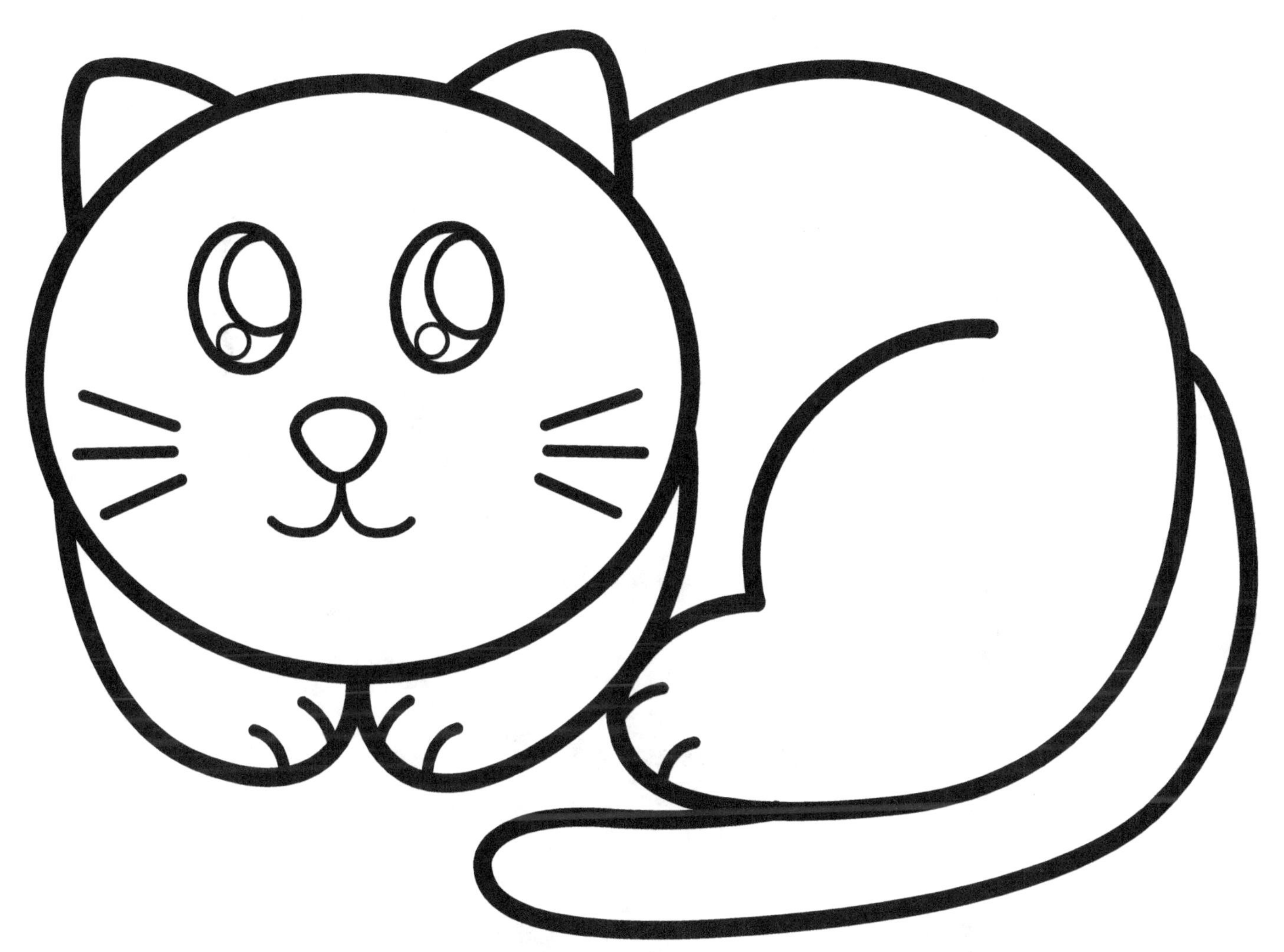

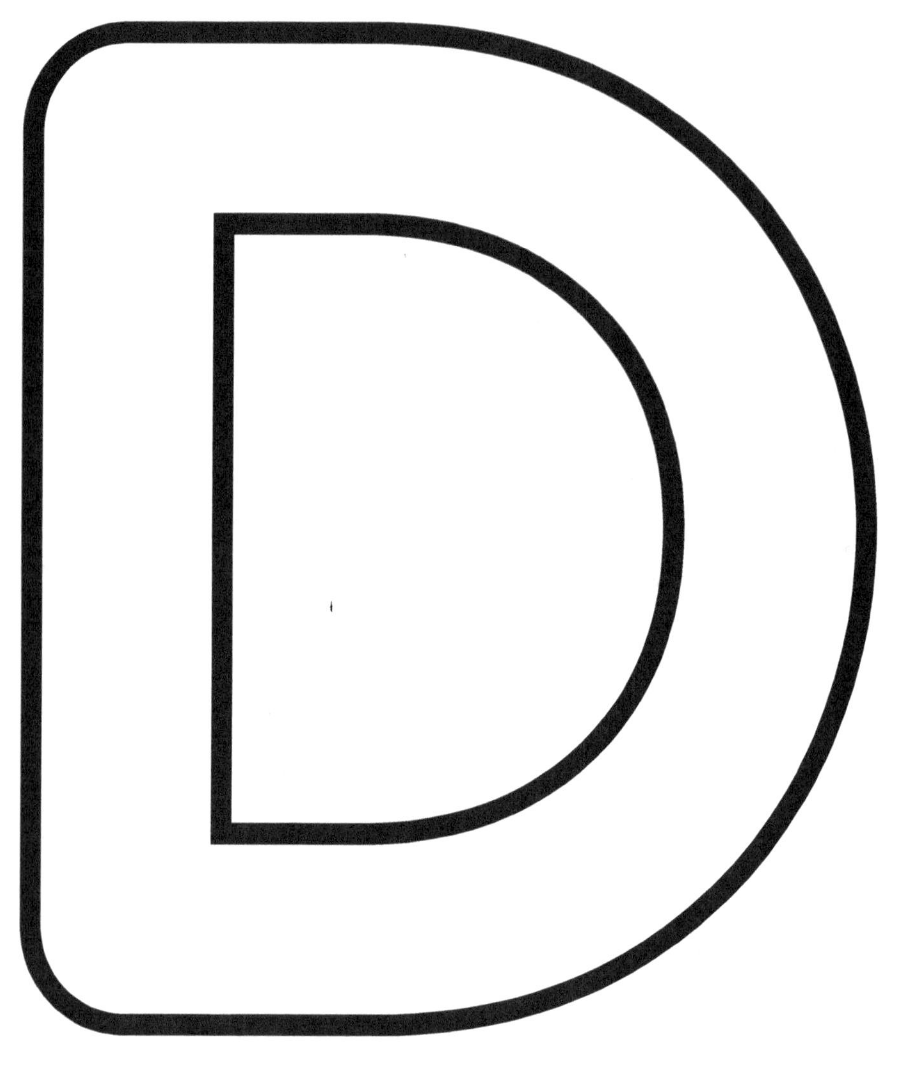

# DUCK

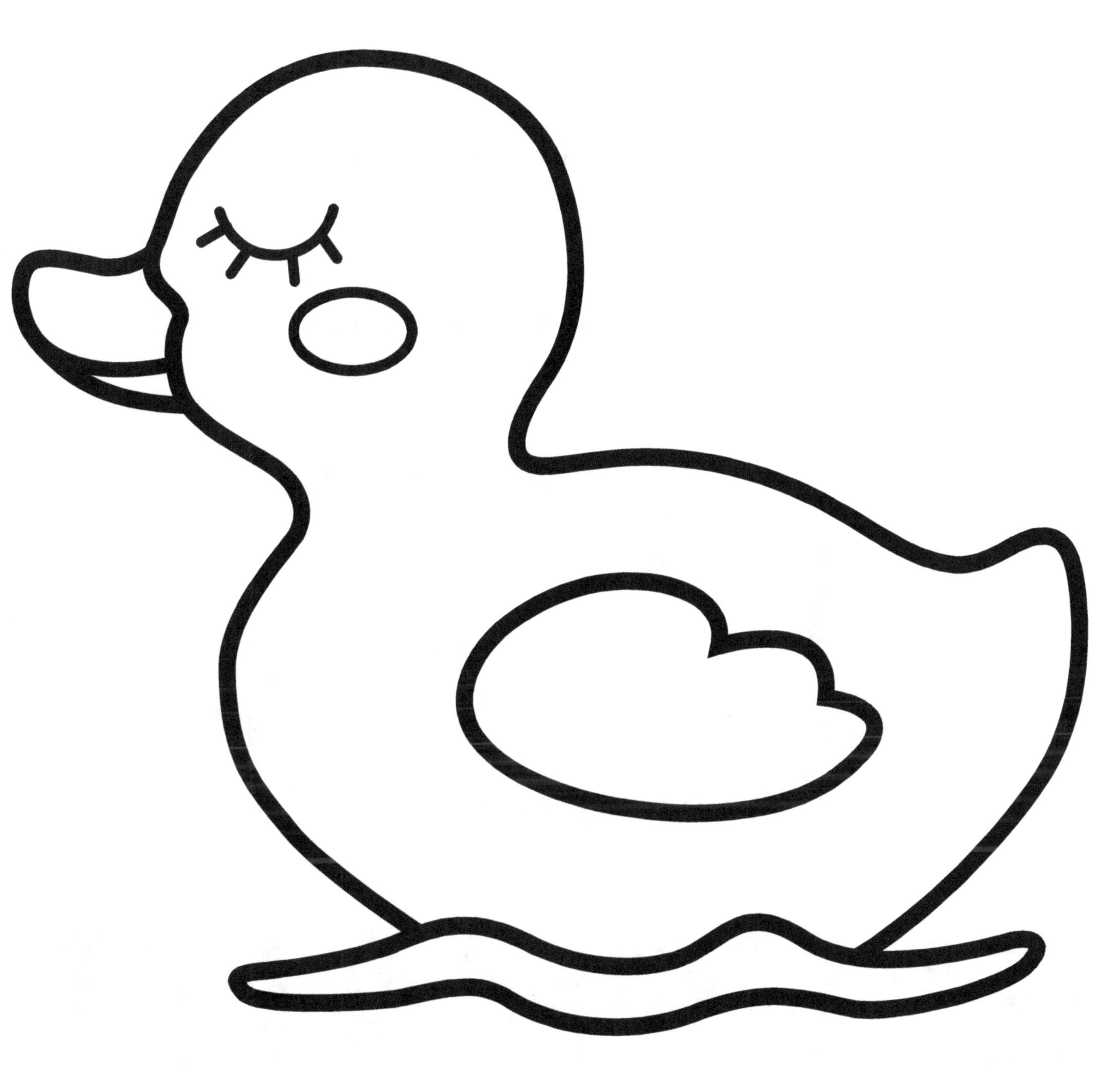

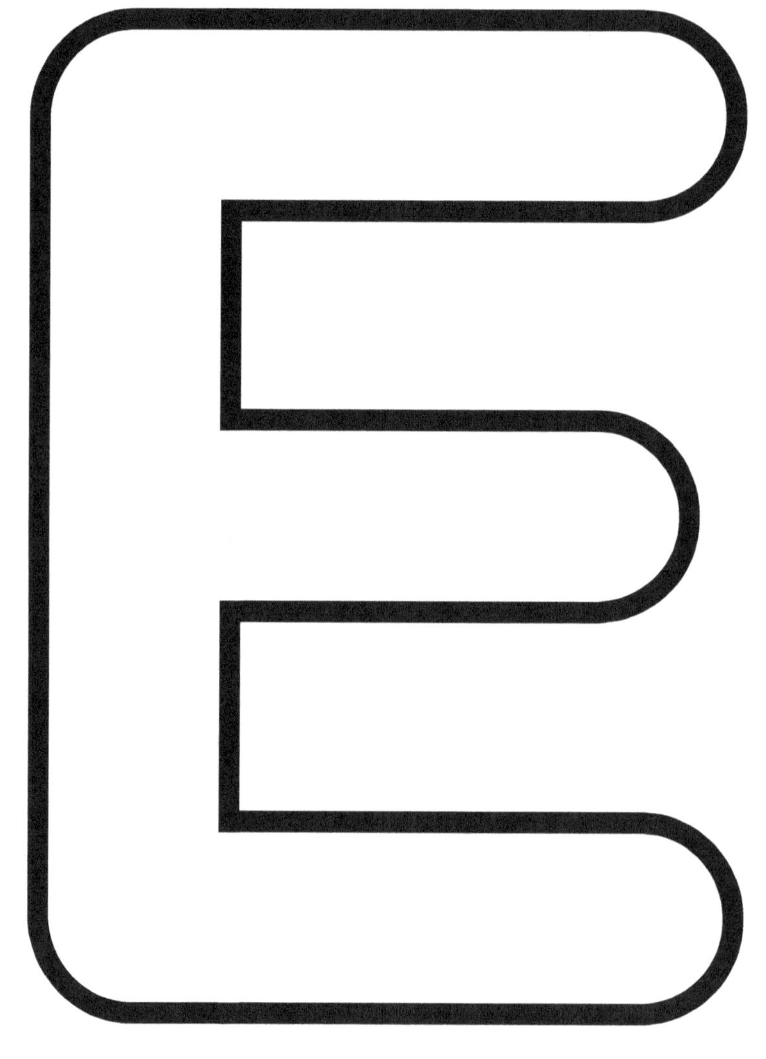

ELEPHANT

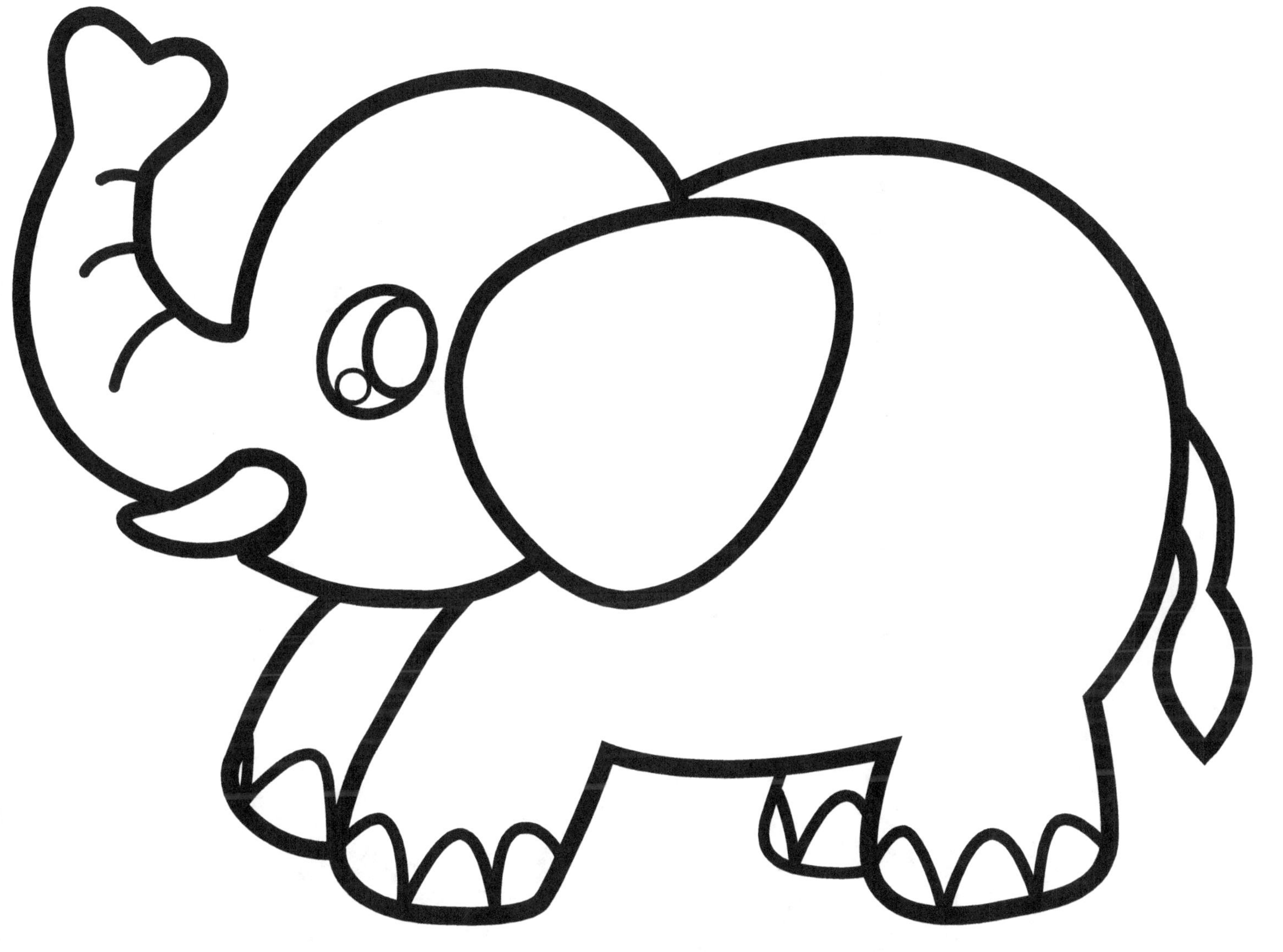

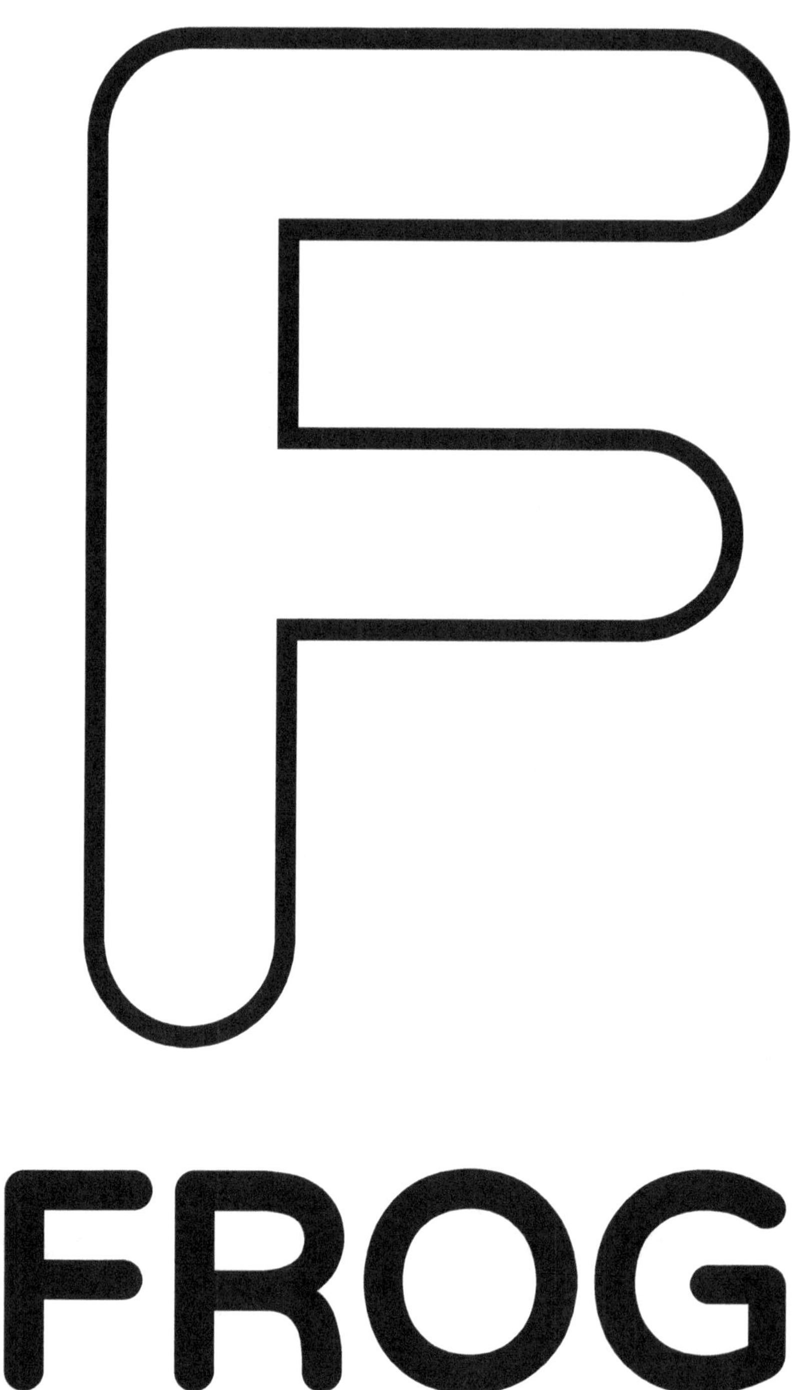

FROG

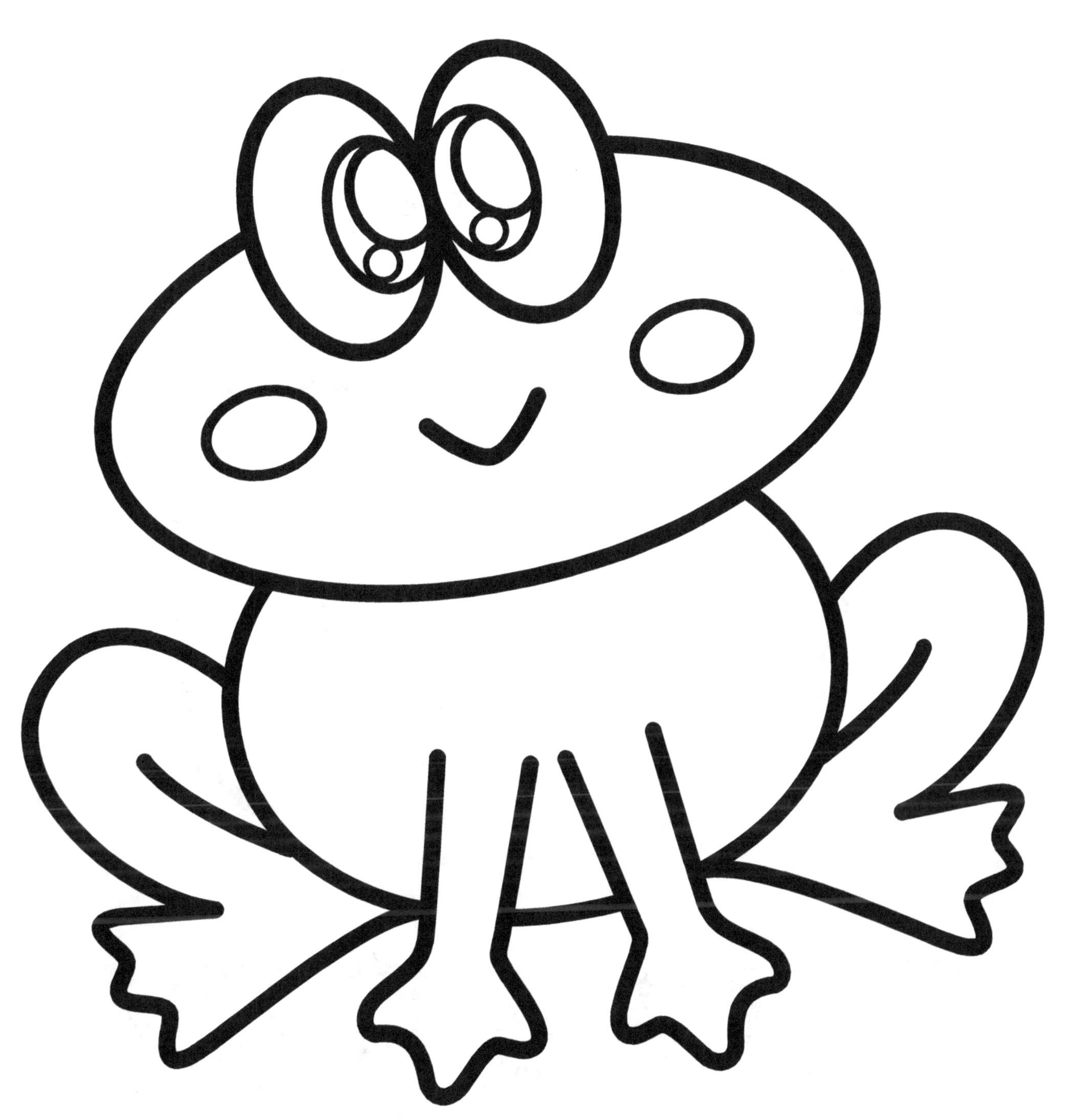

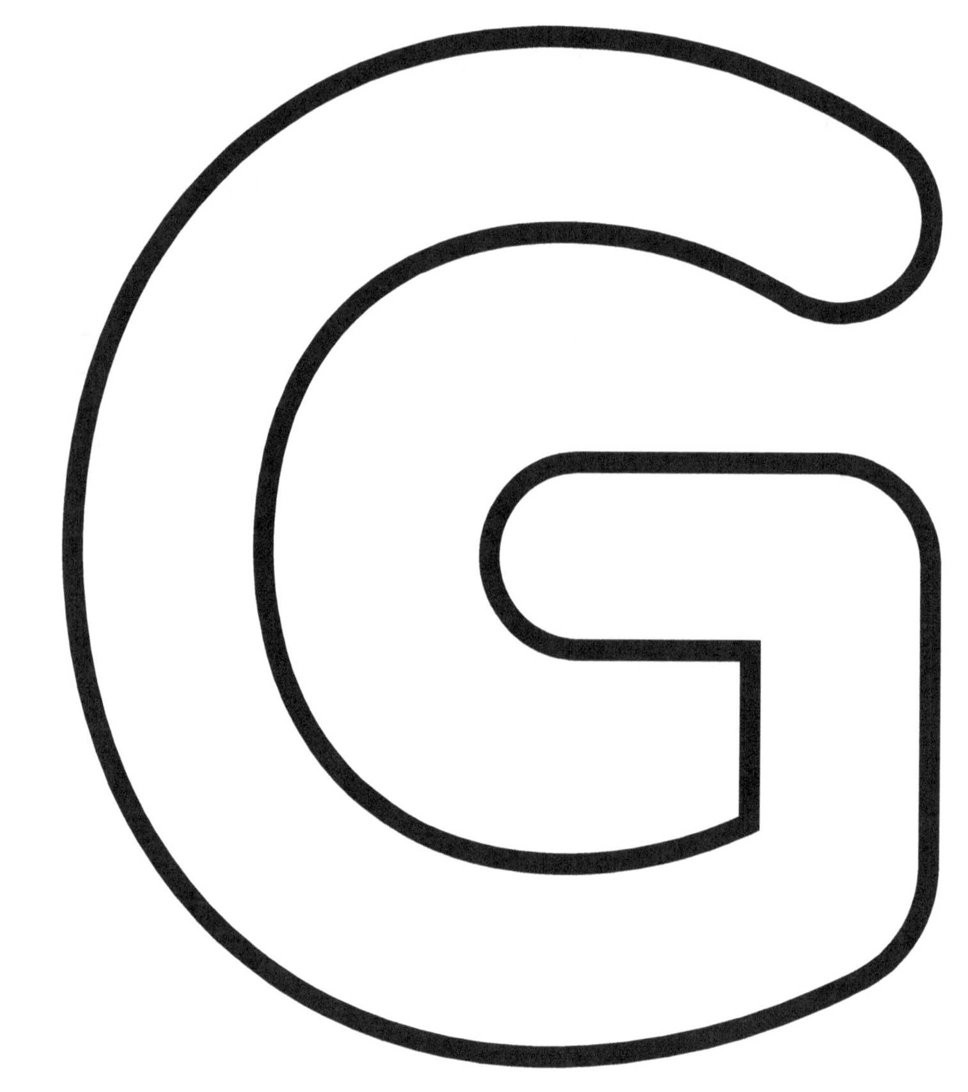

GIRAFFE

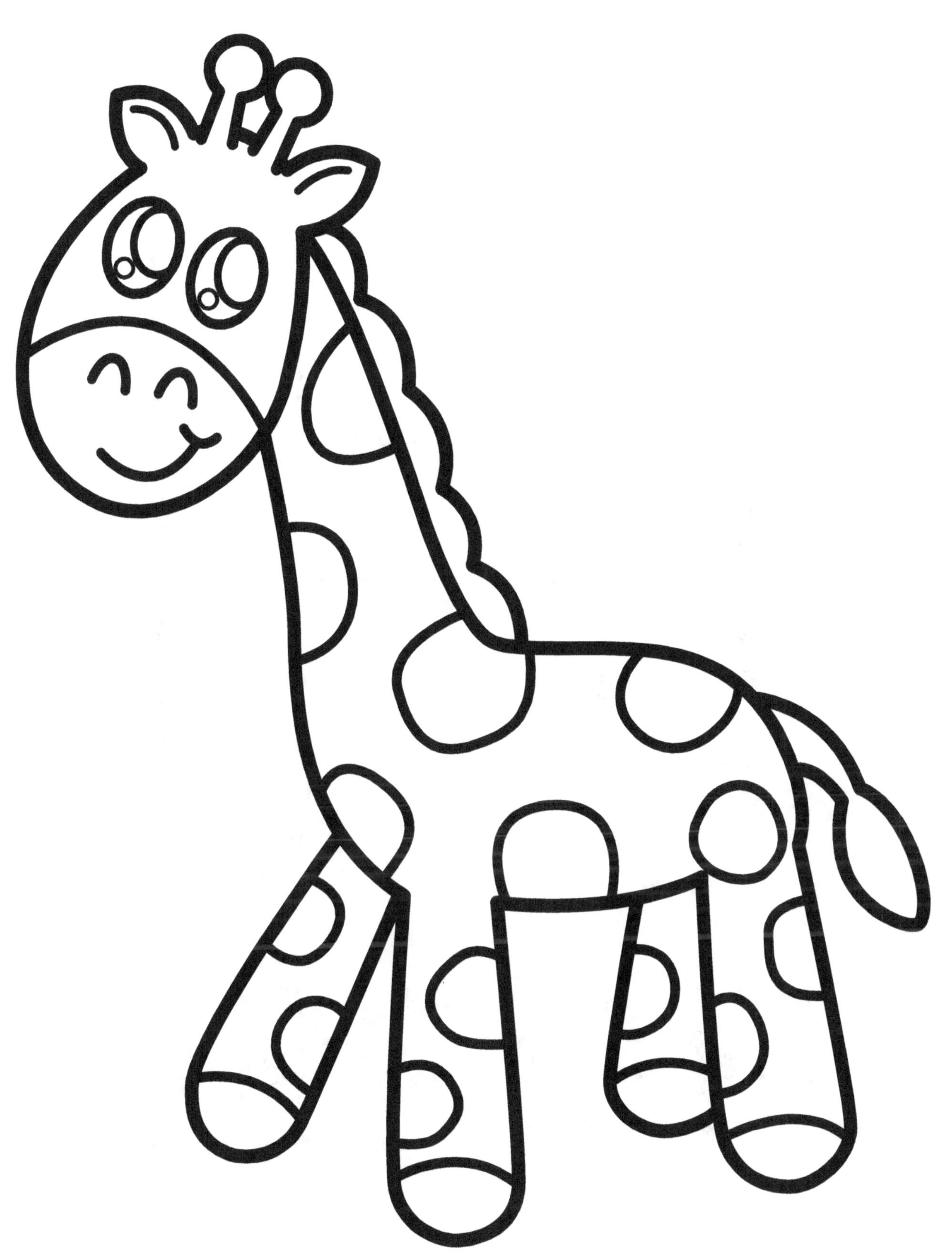

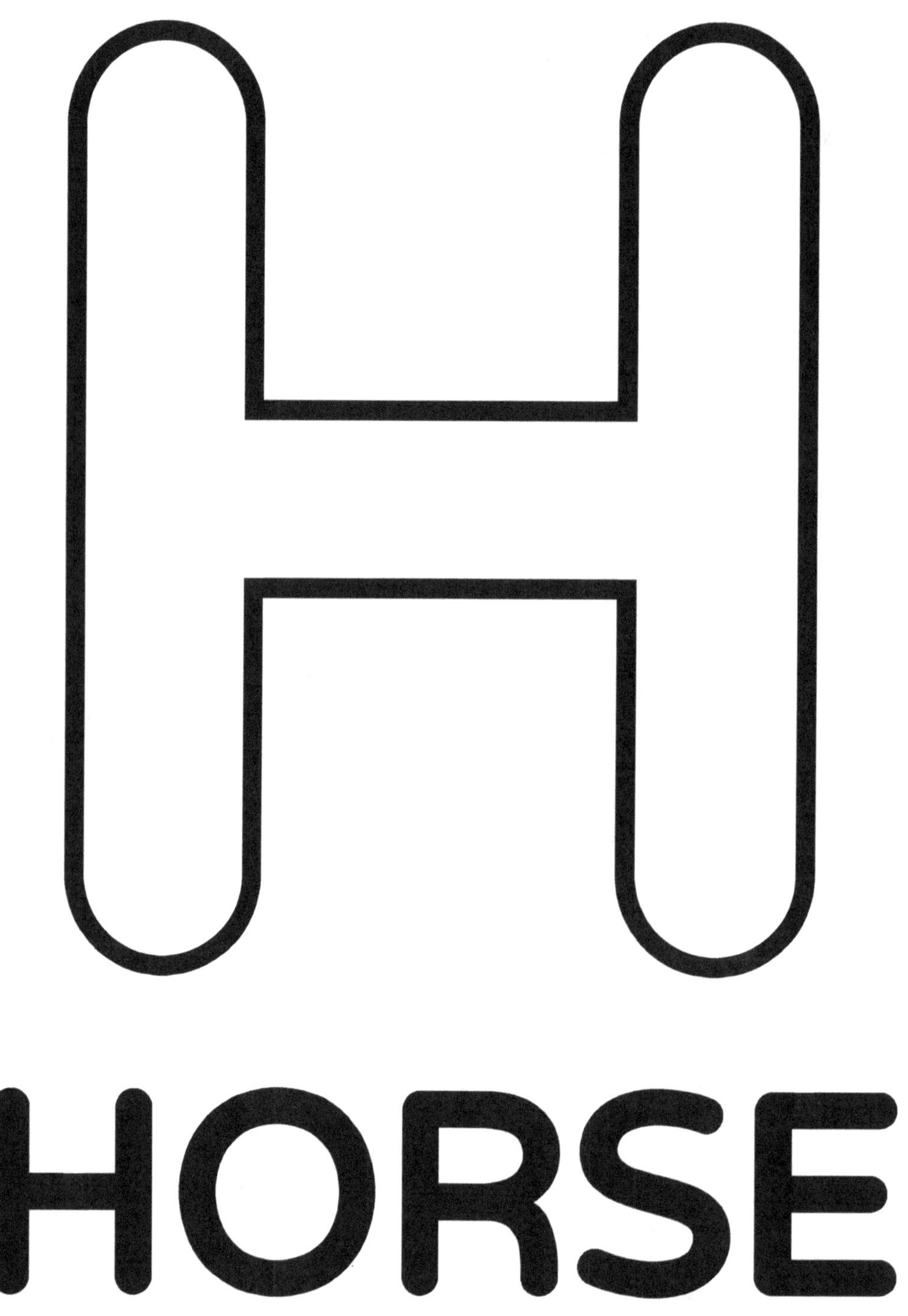

HORSE

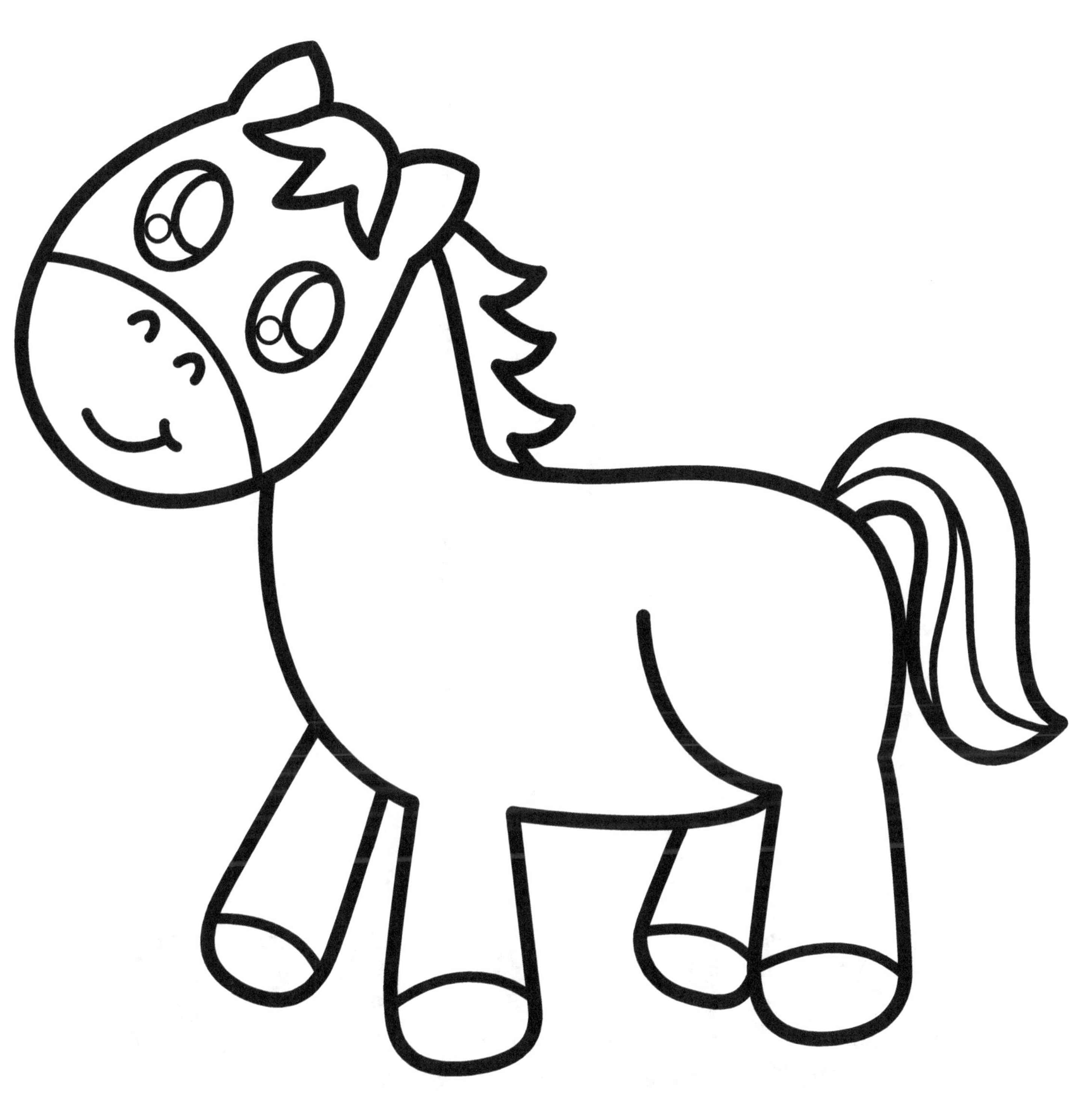

# IGUANA

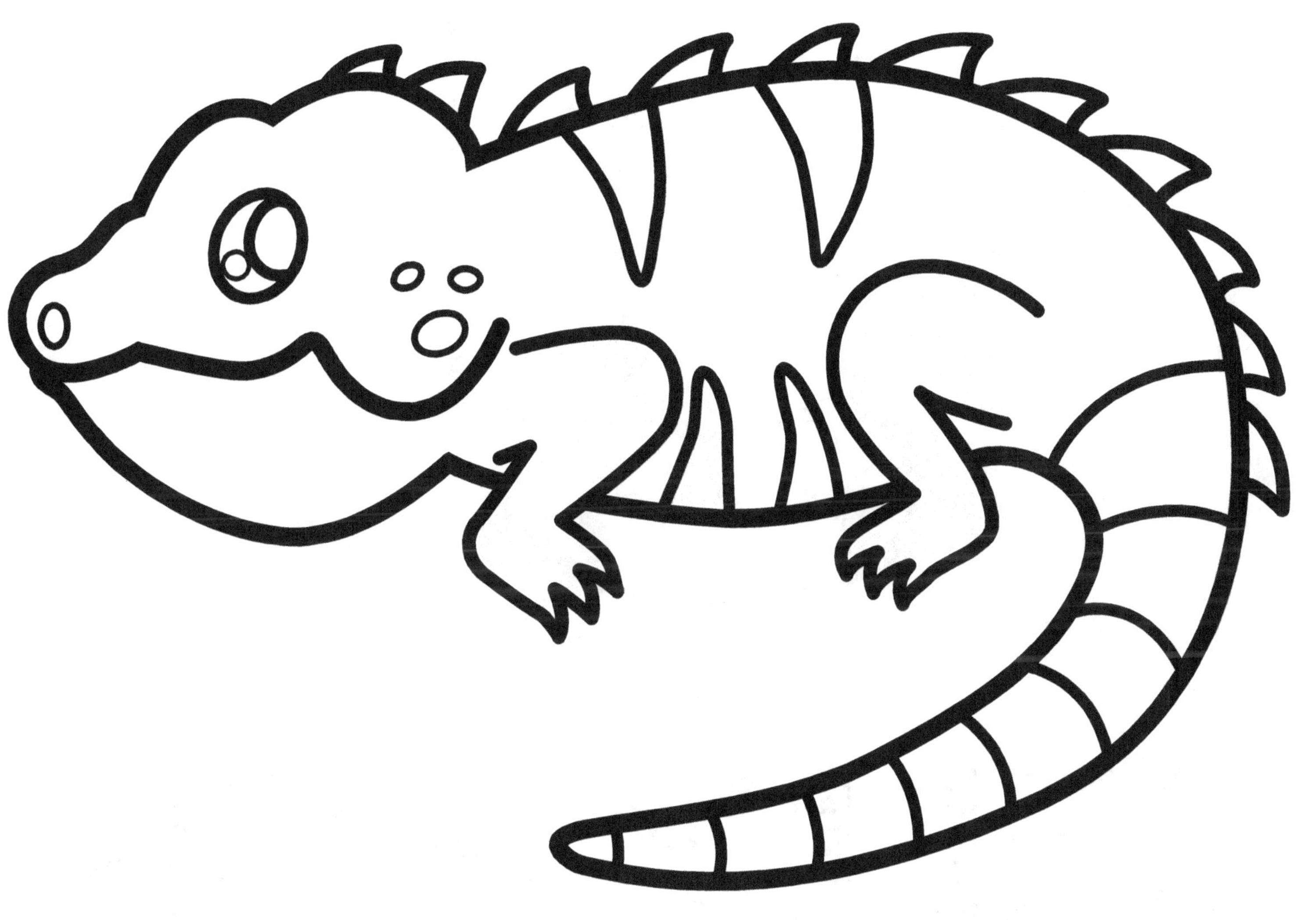

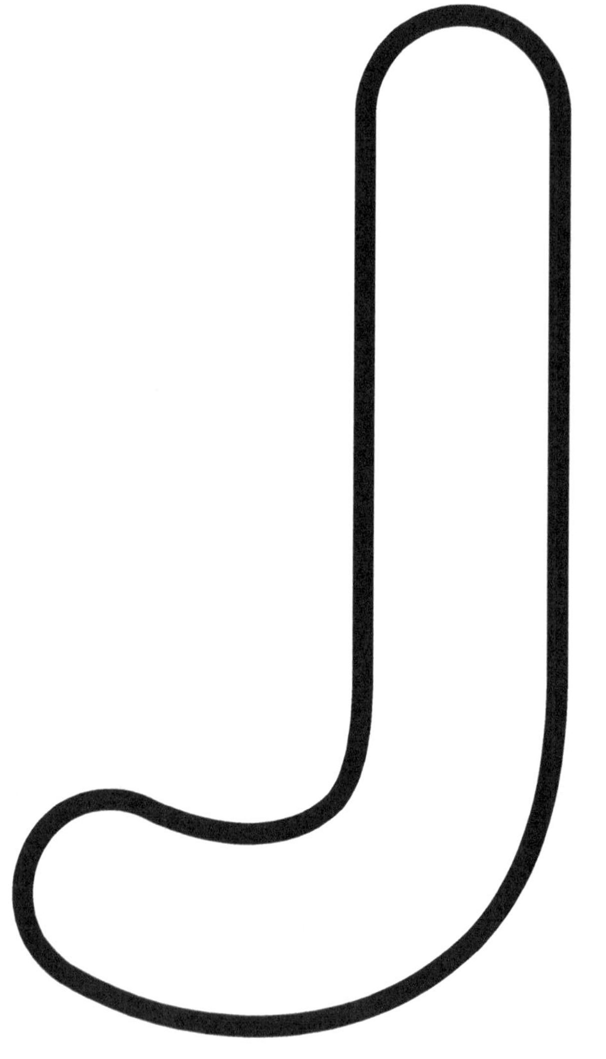

# JELLY FISH

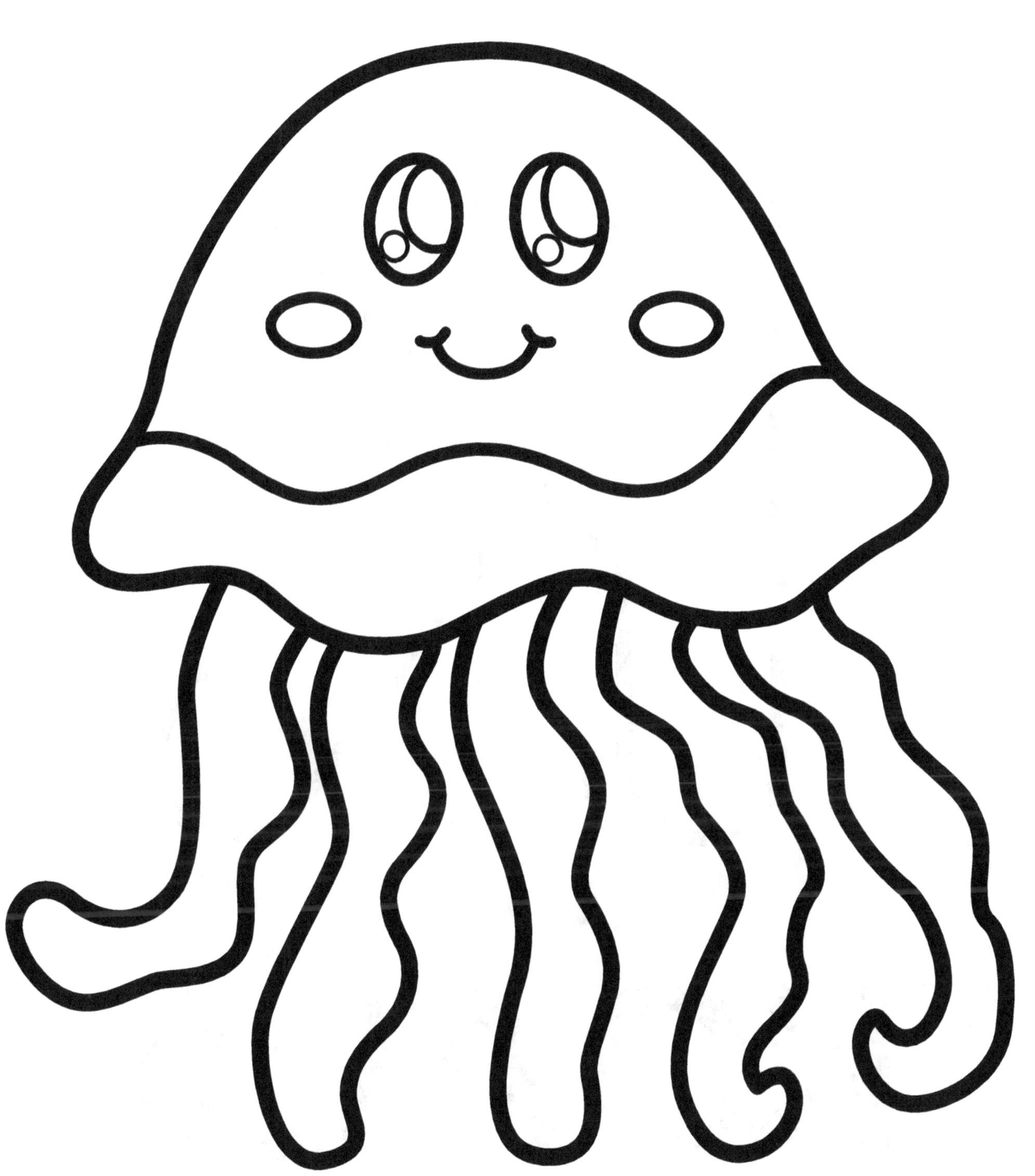

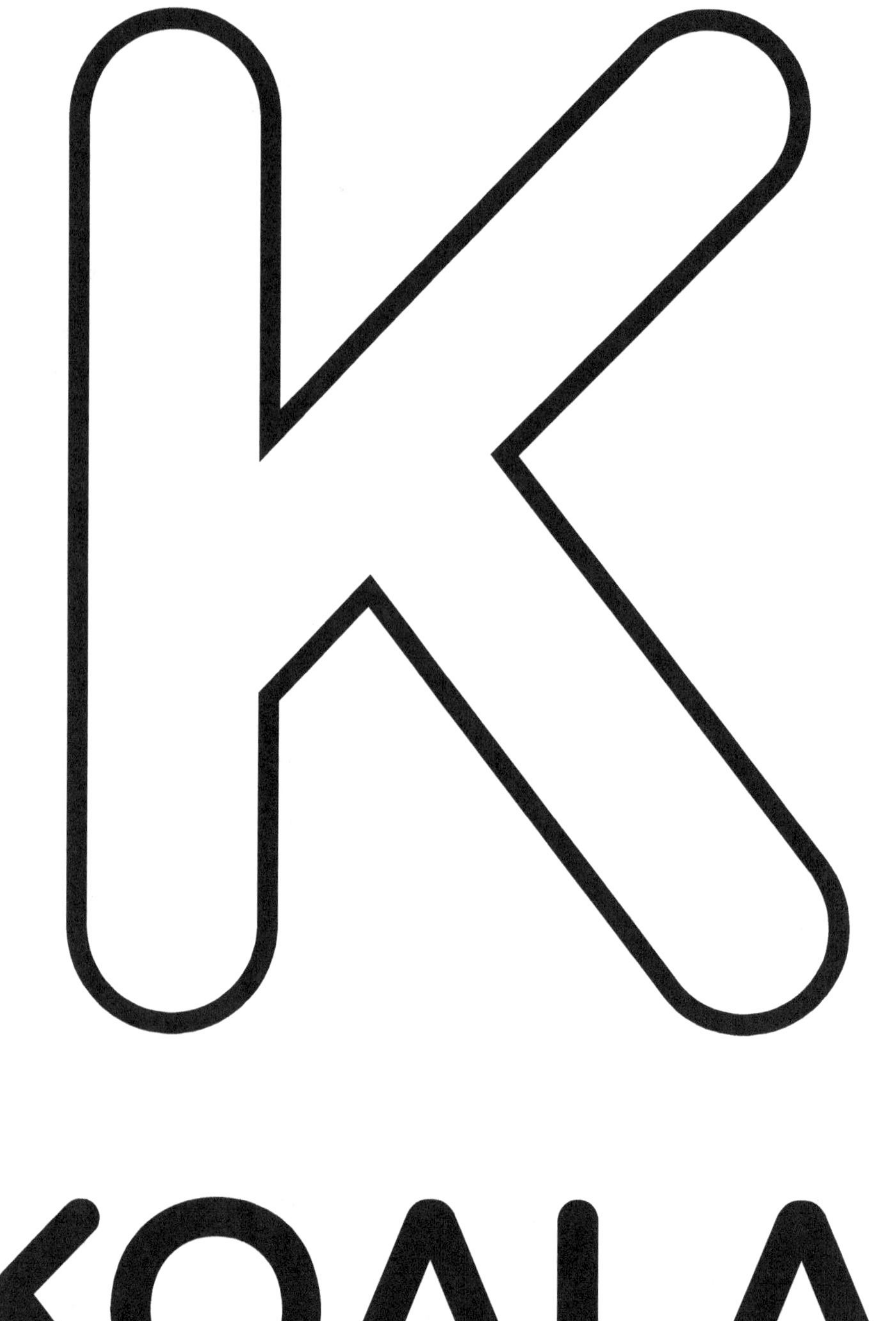
KOALA

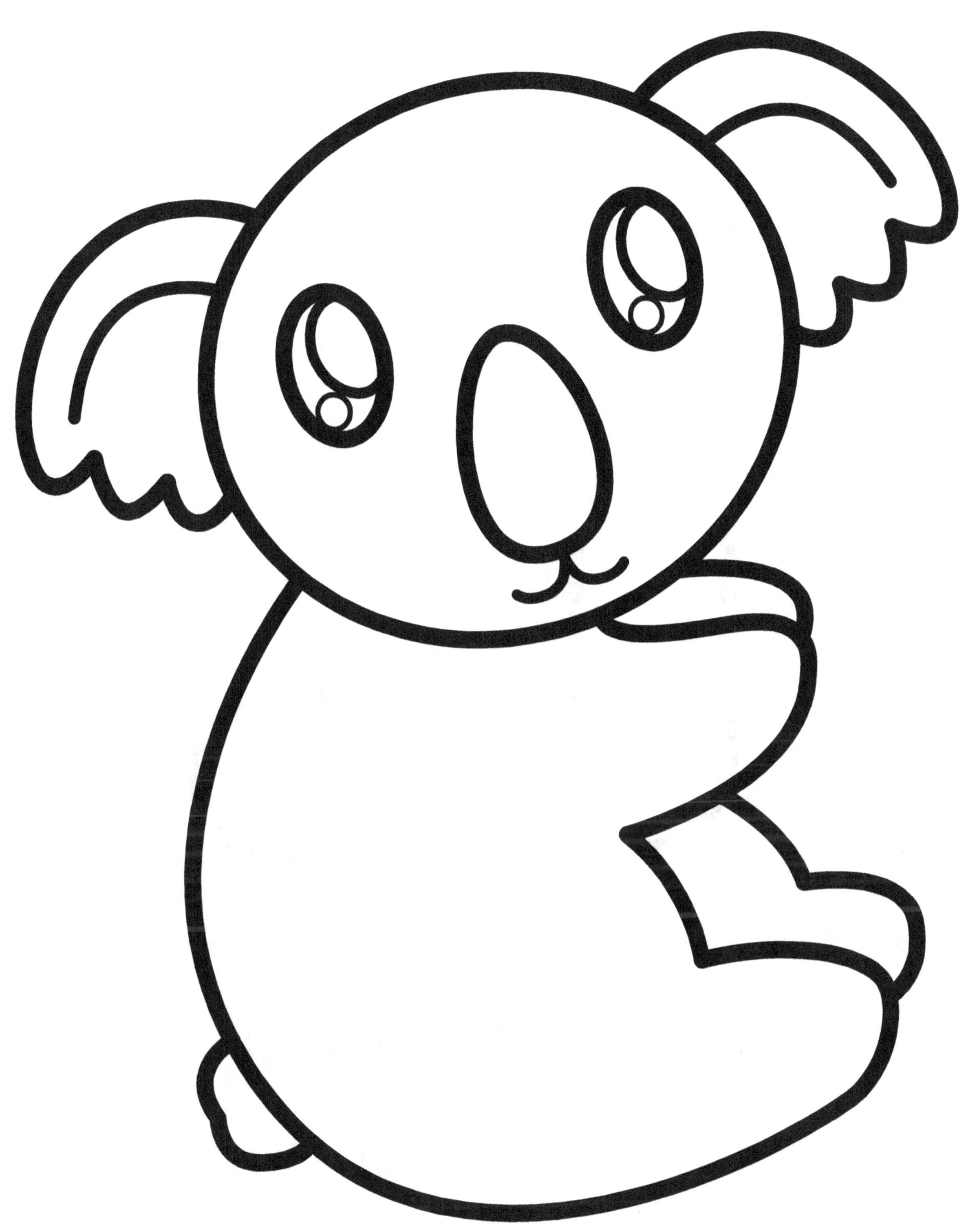

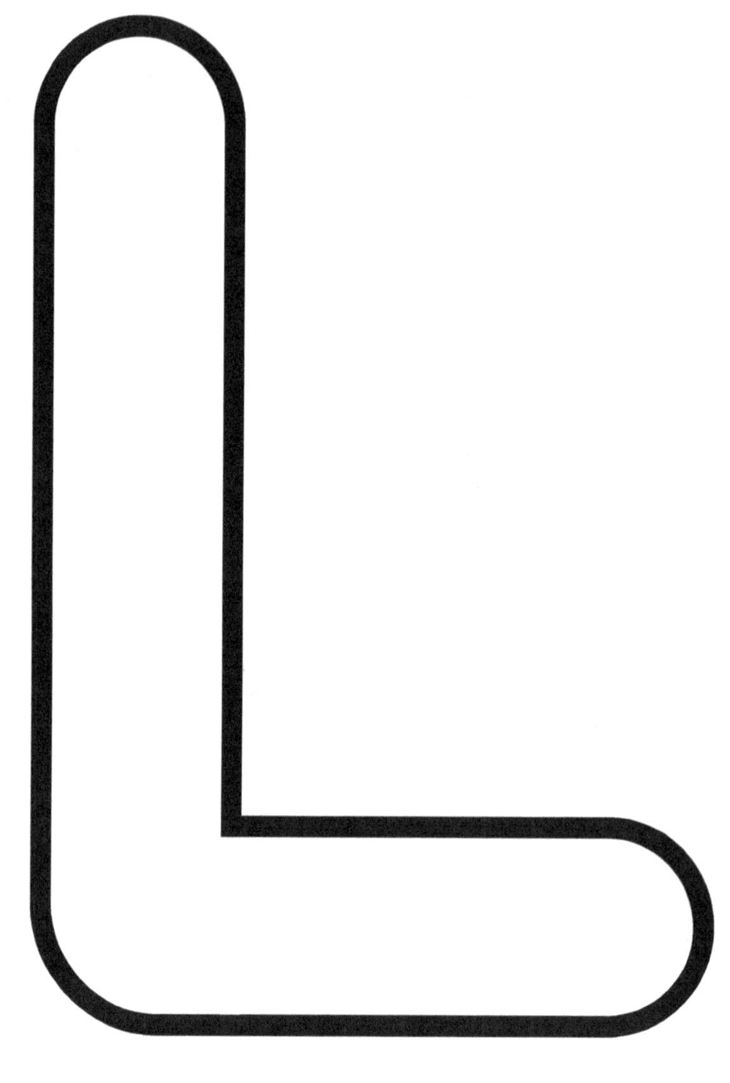

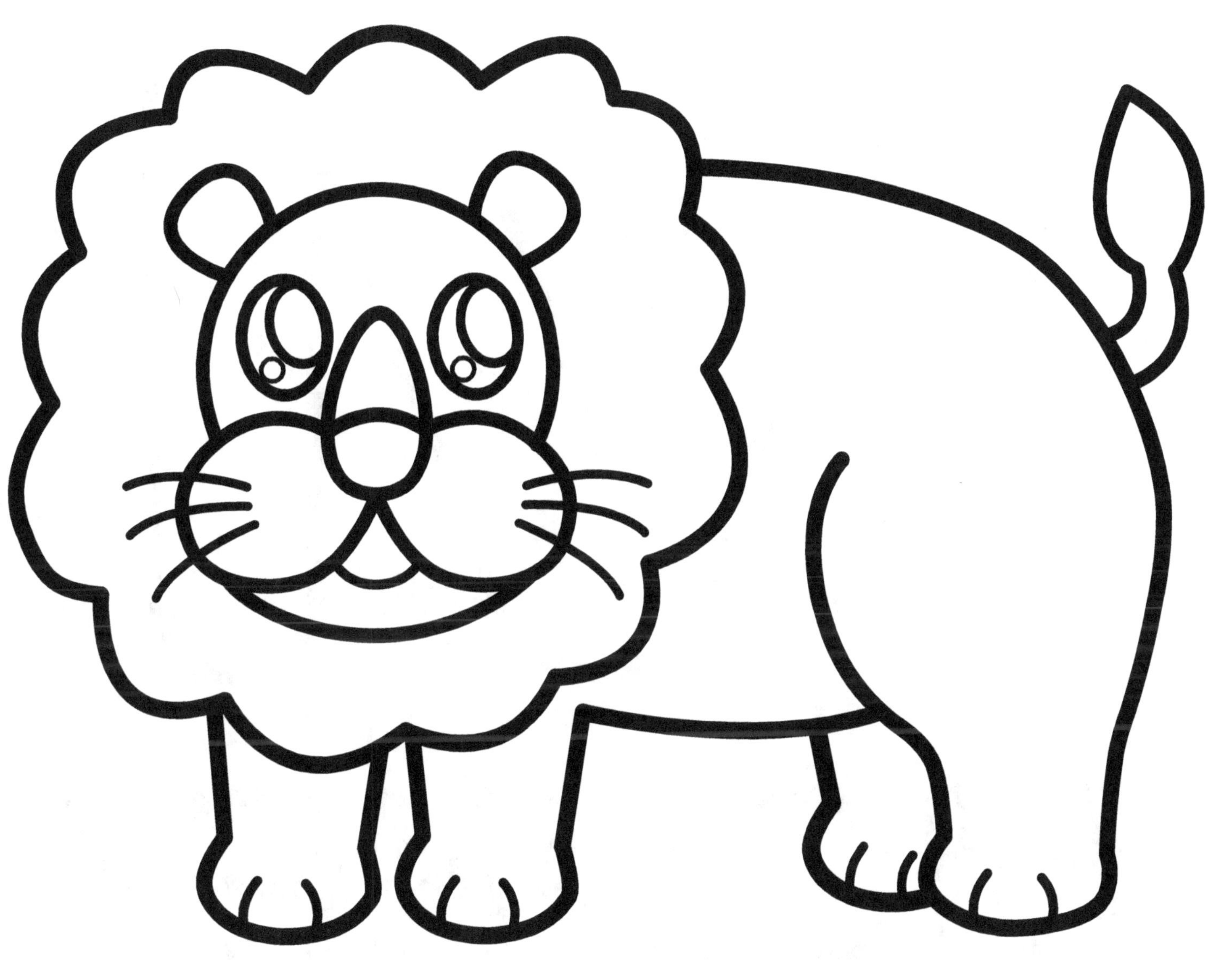

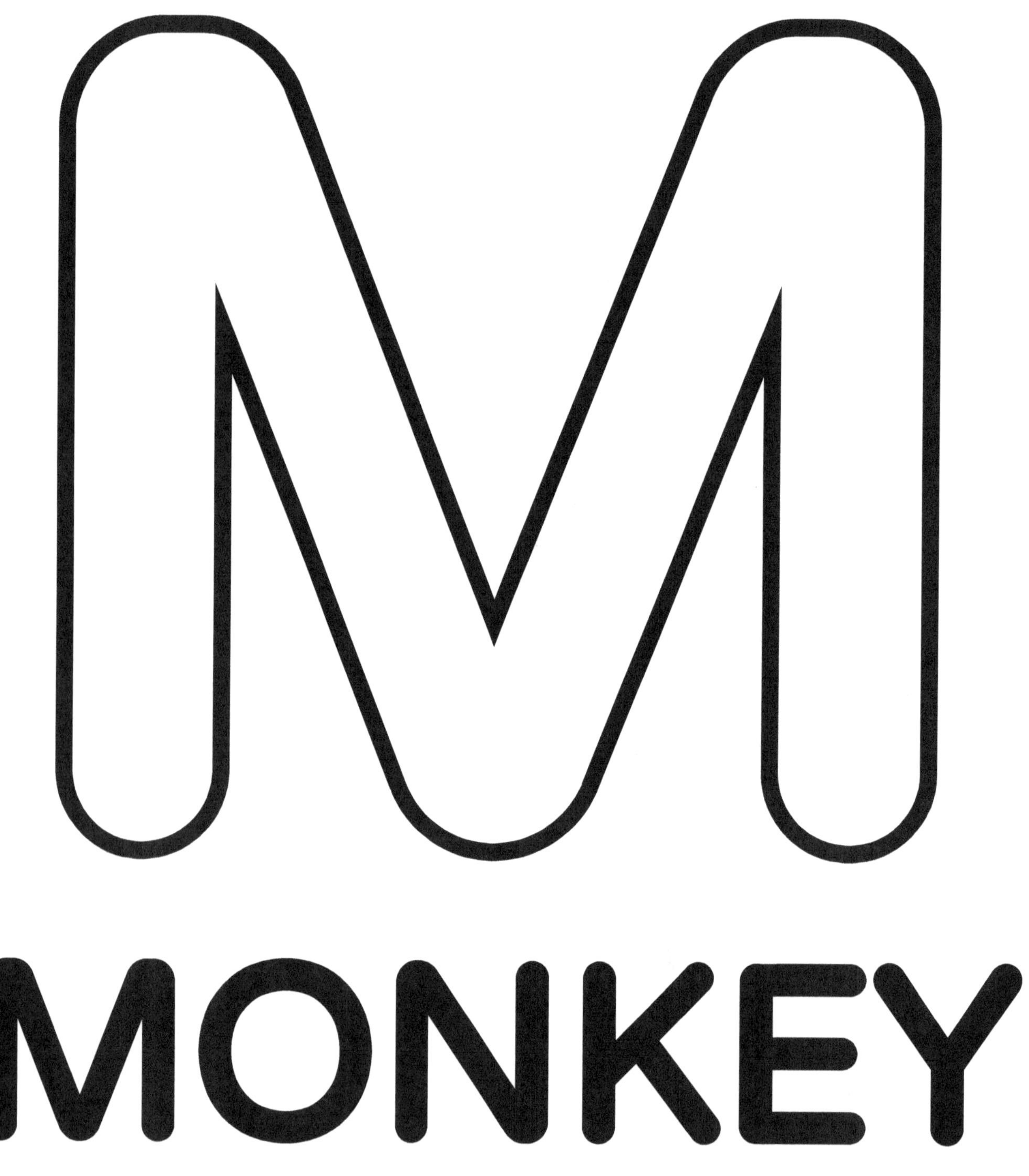

MONKEY

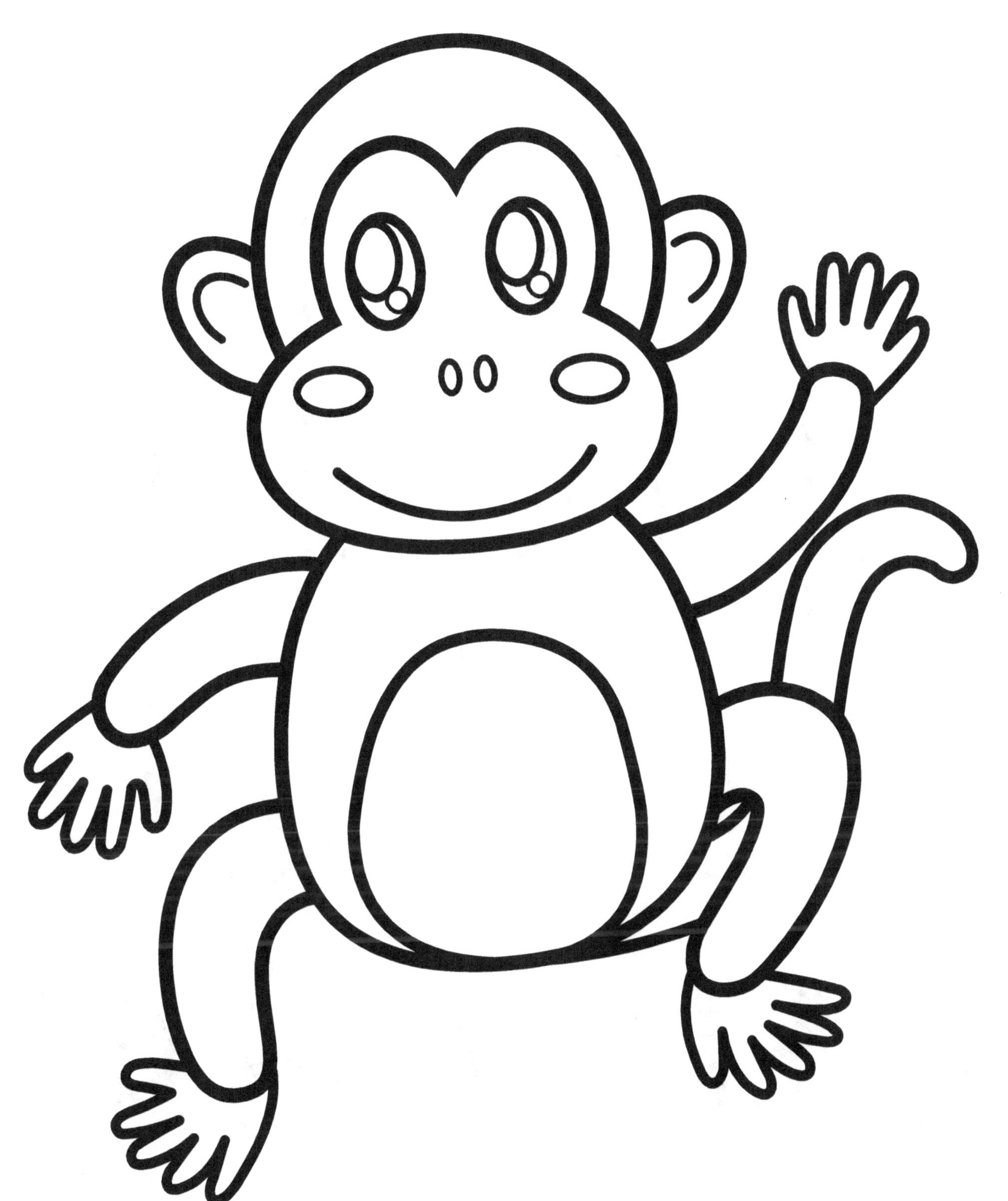

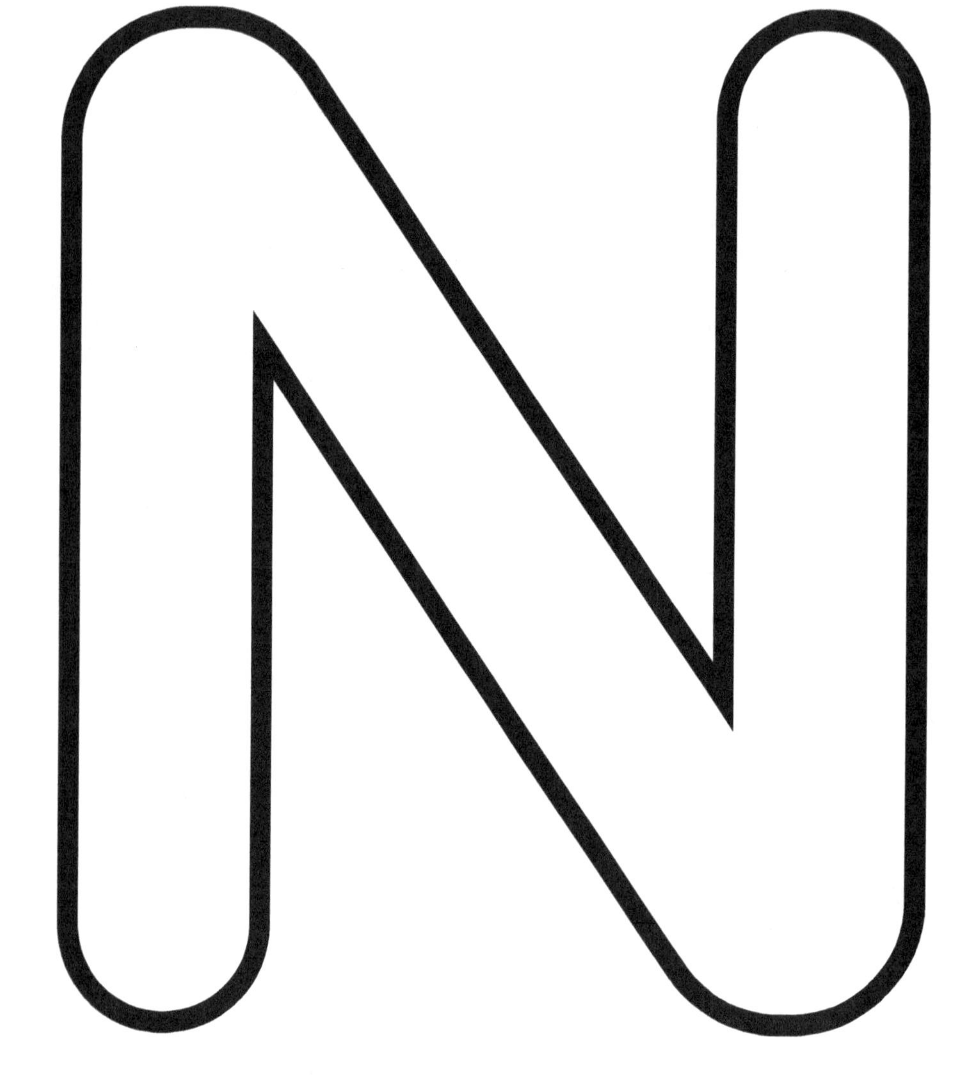

NAR WHAL

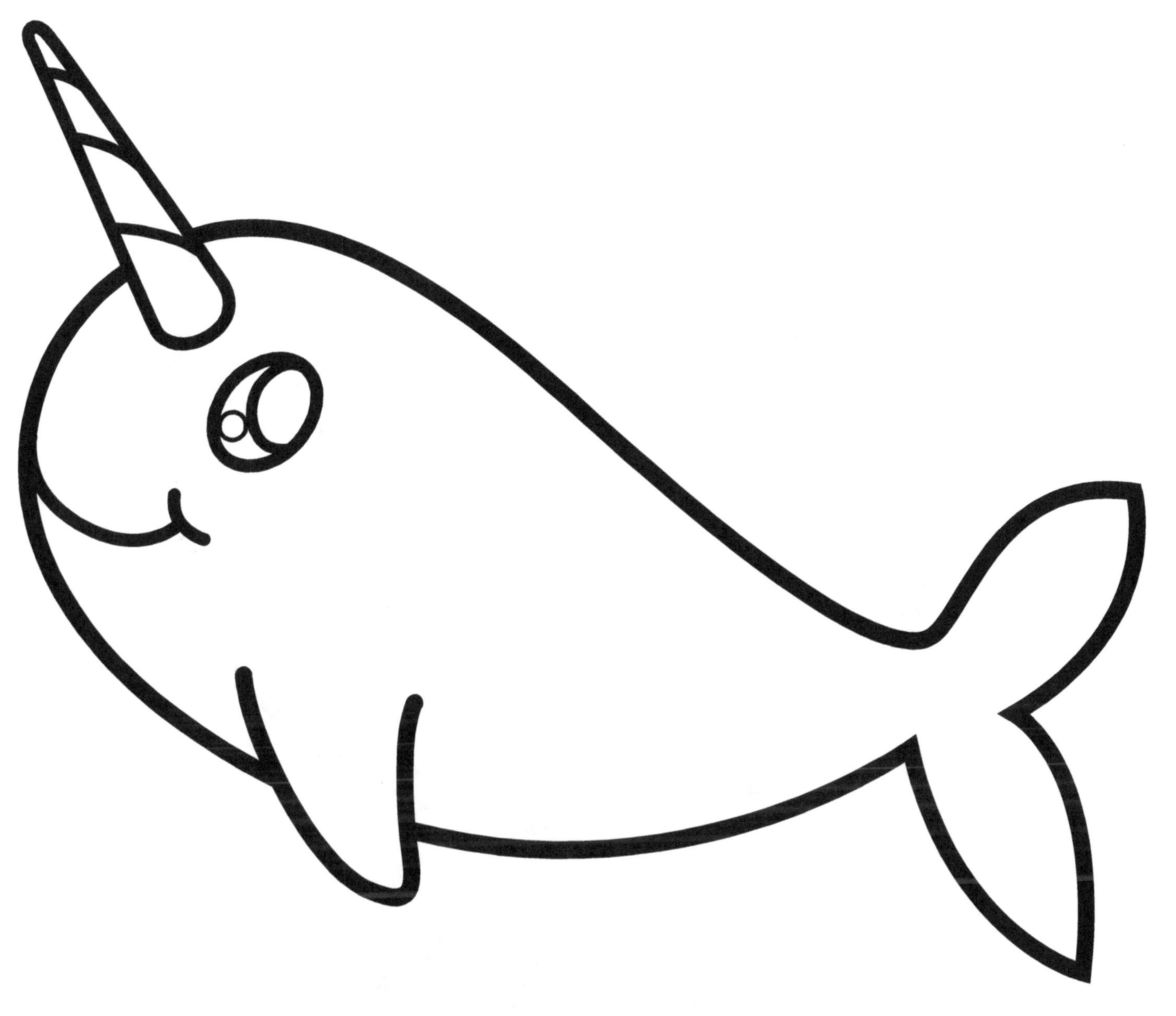

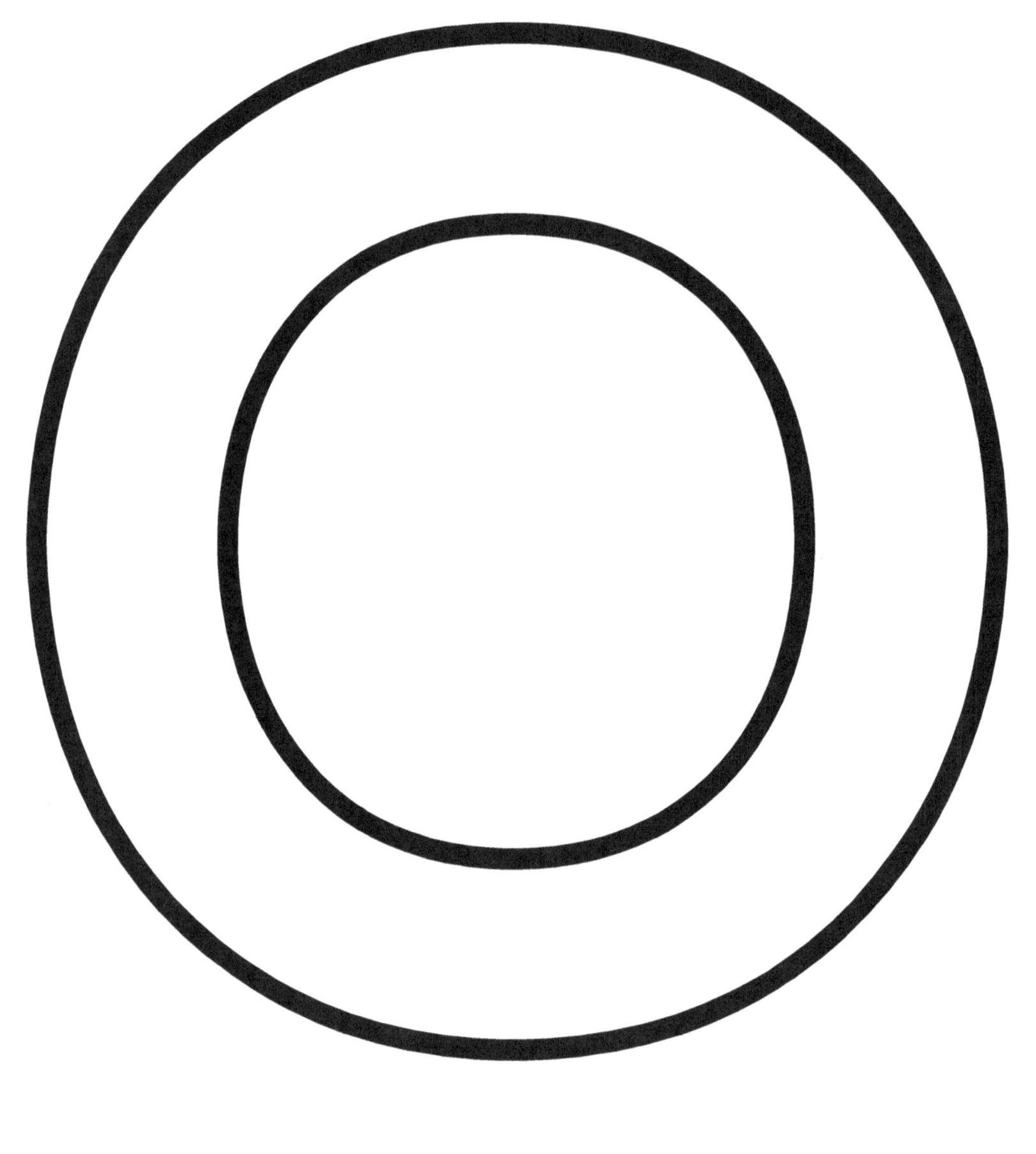

# OWL

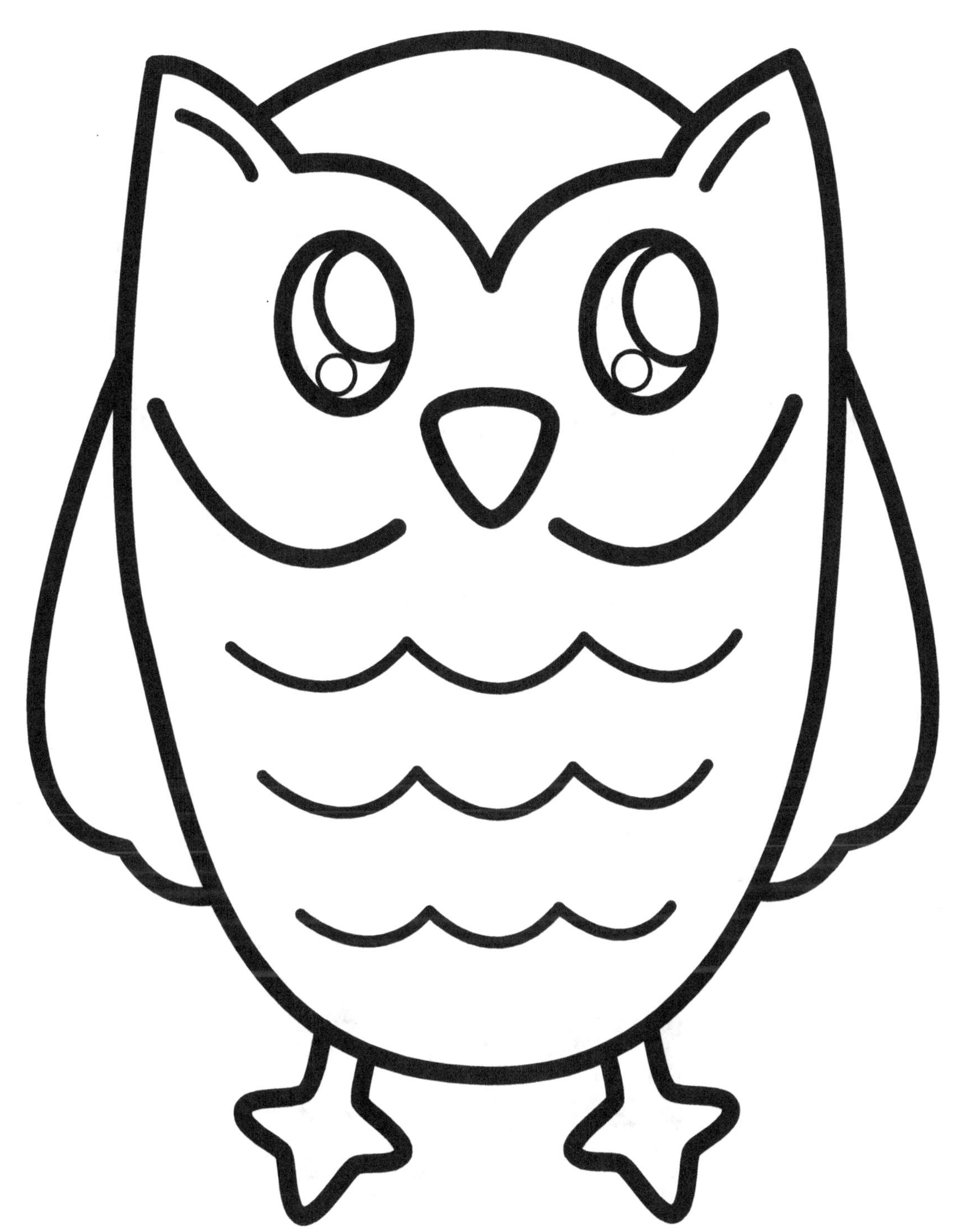

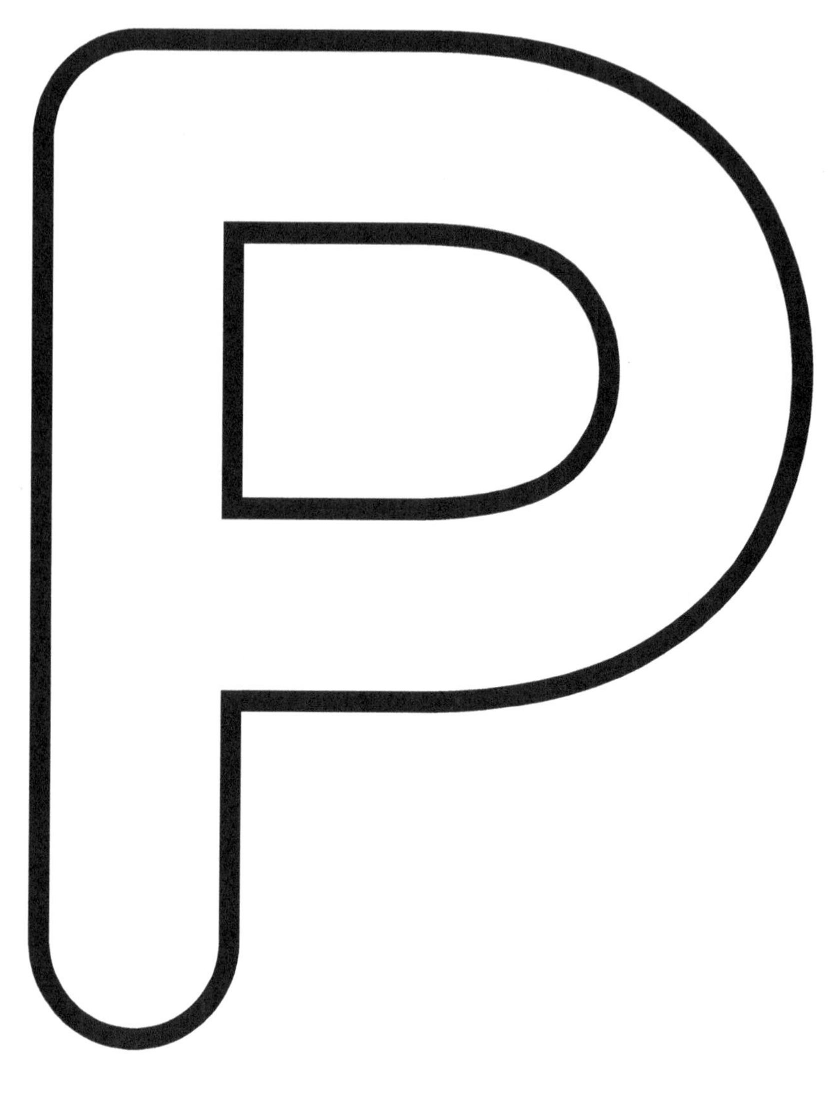

PIG

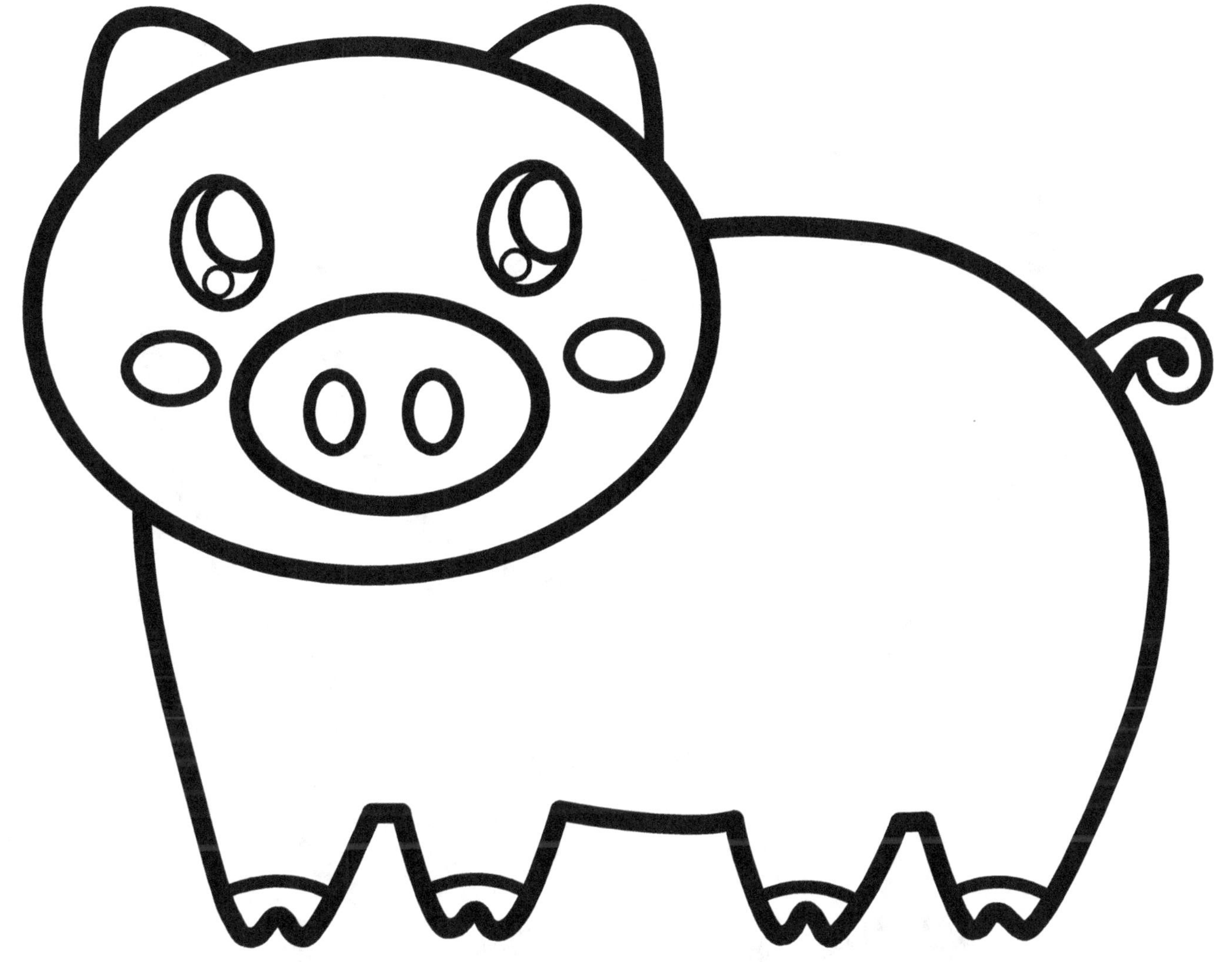

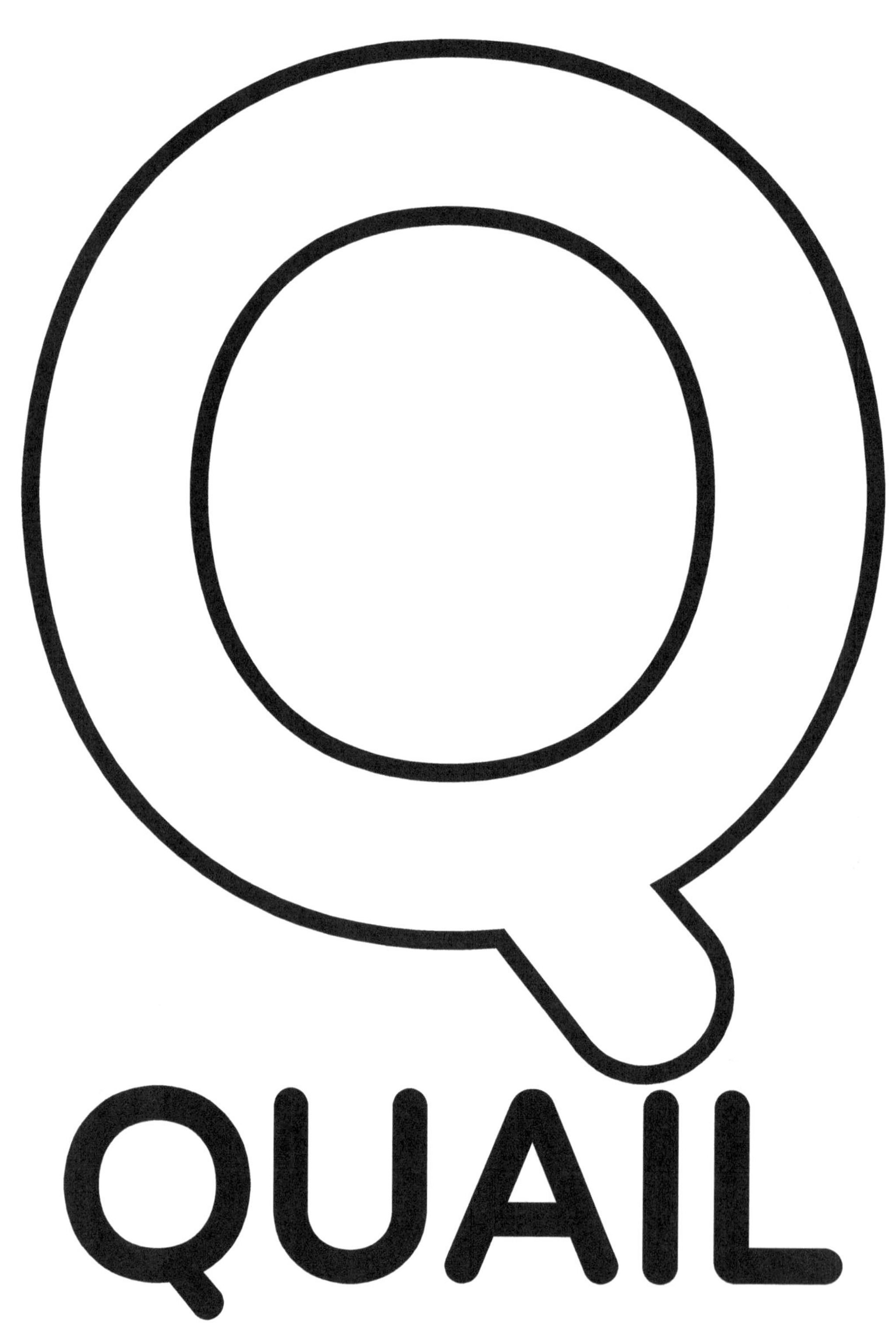
QUAIL

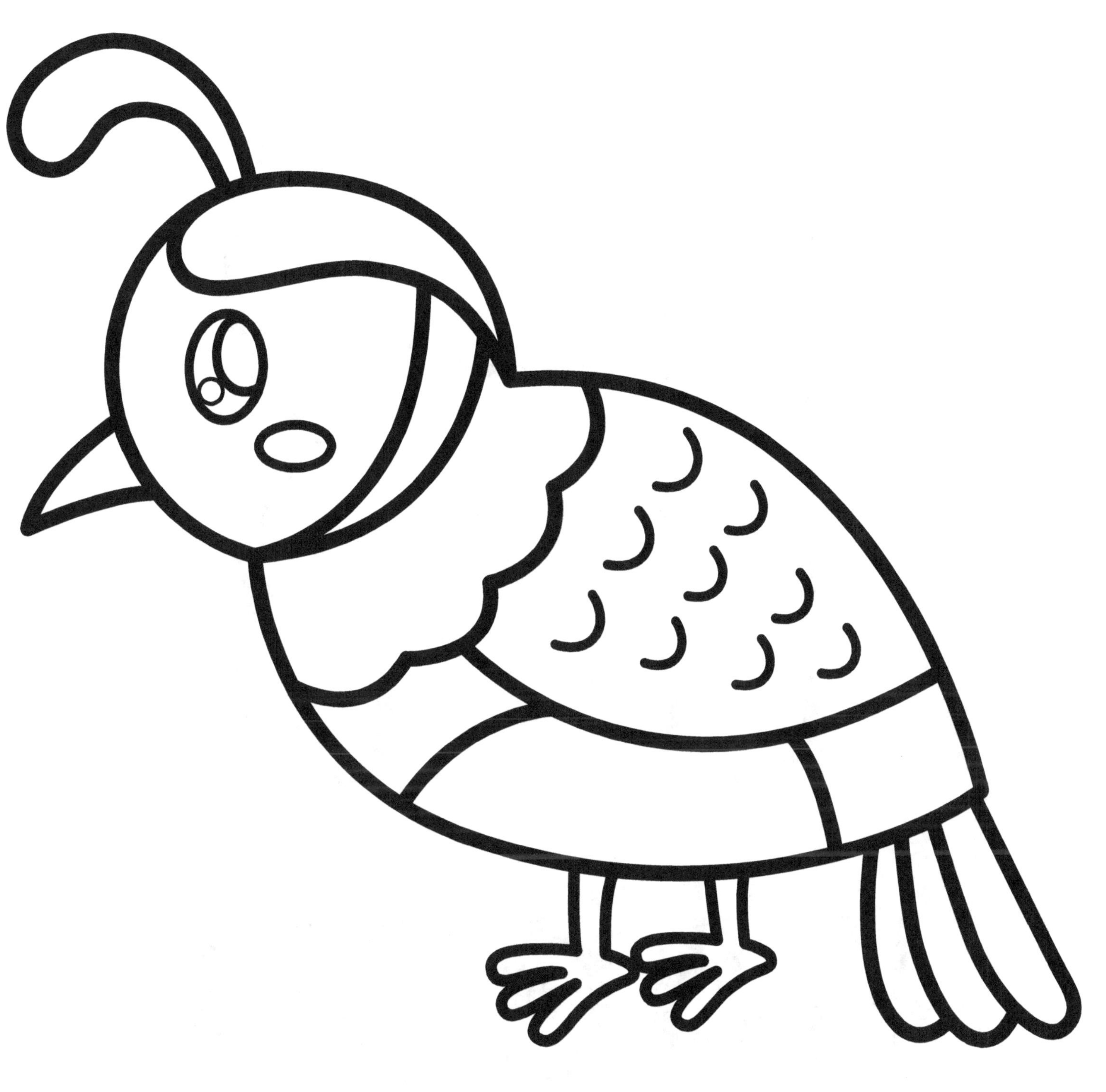

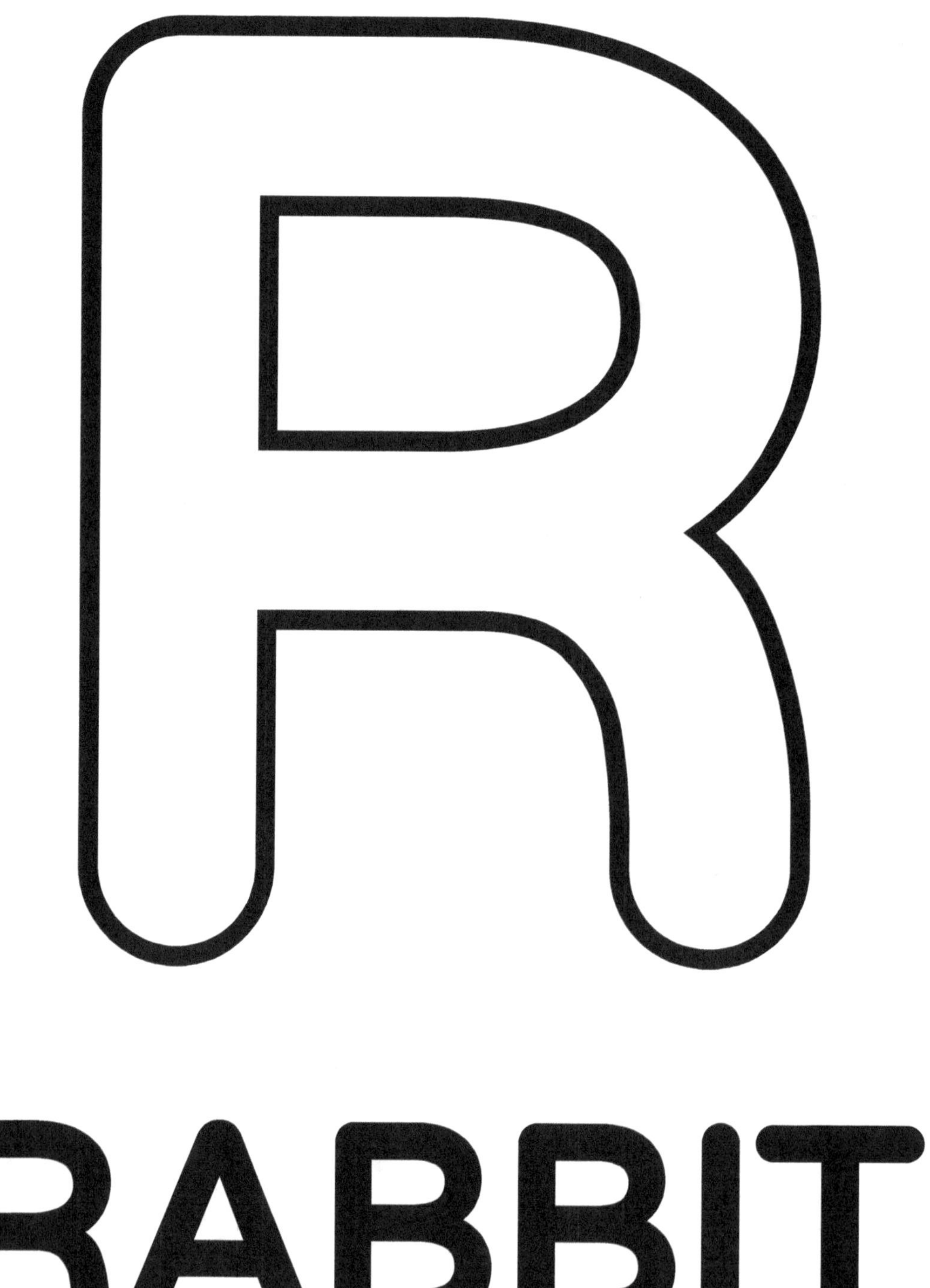

RABBIT

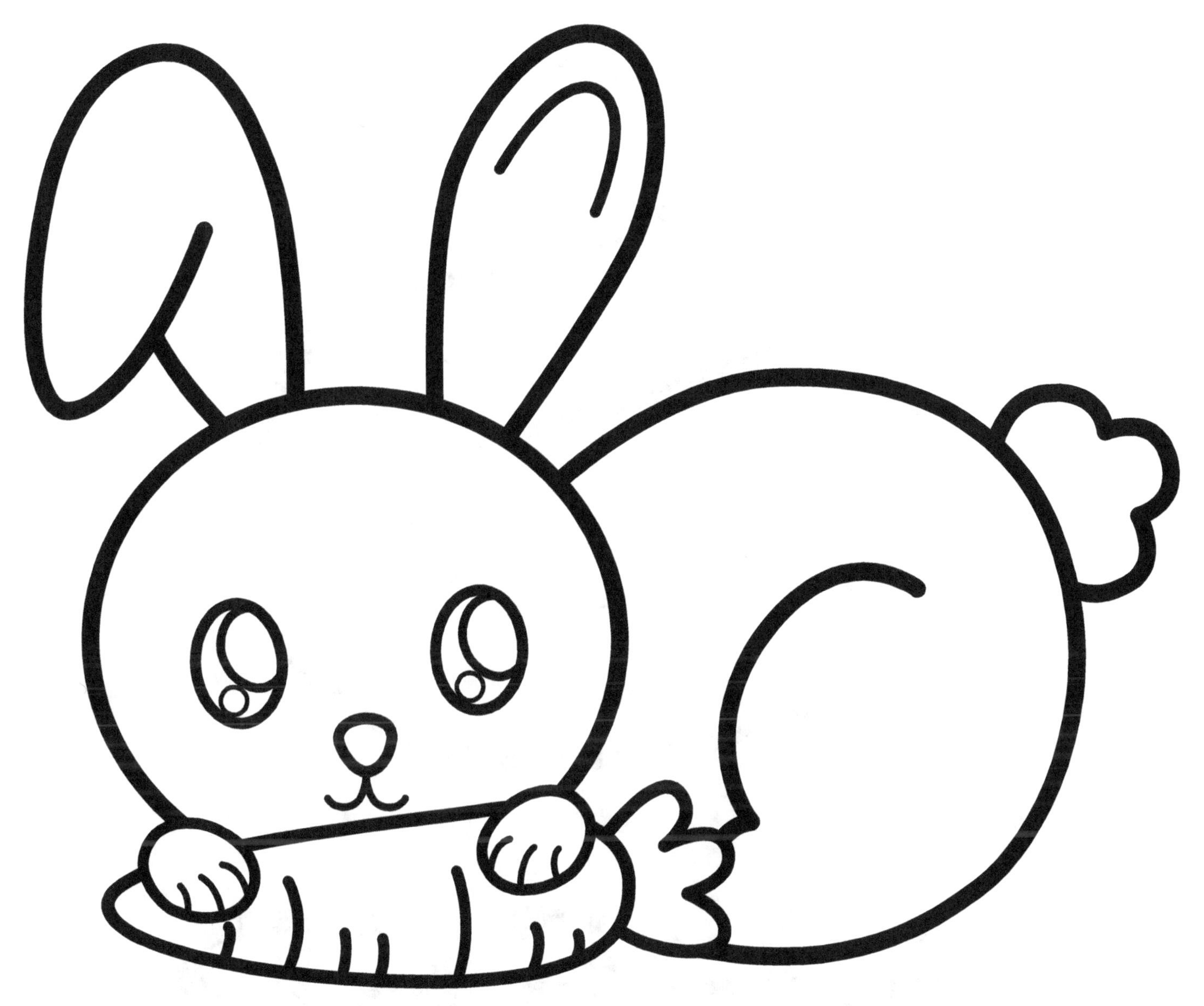

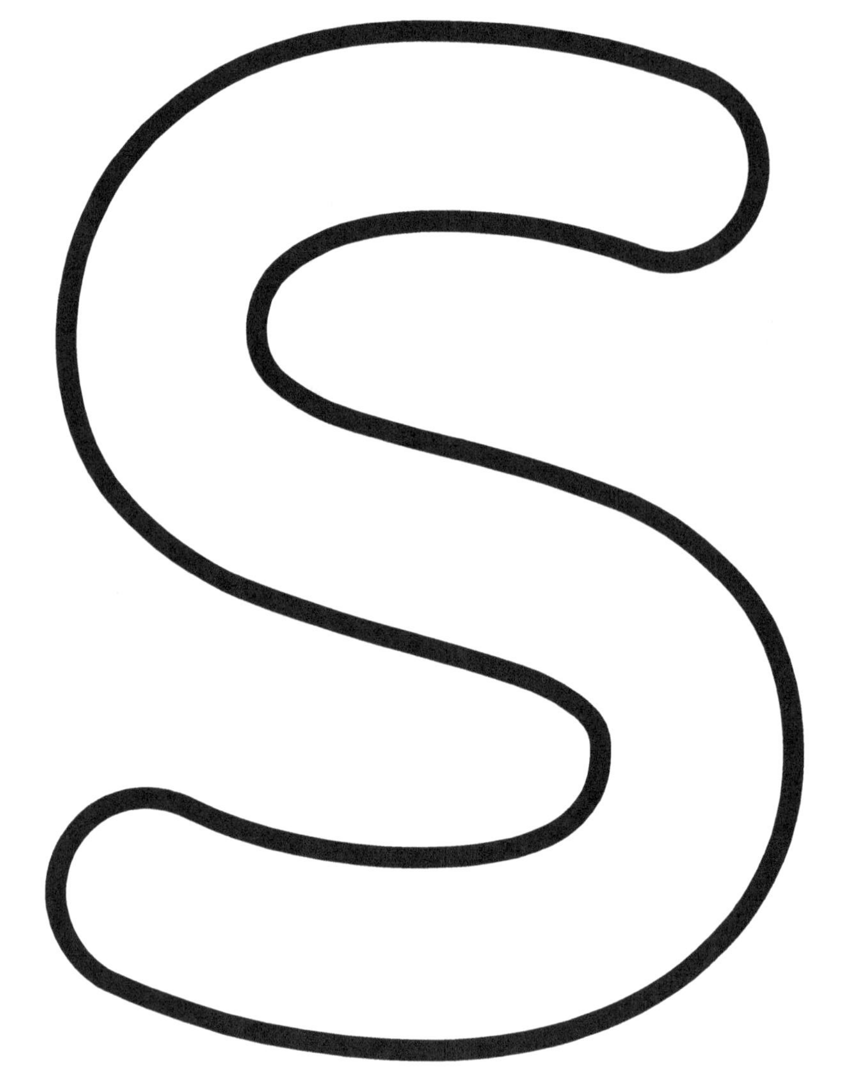

# SHEEP

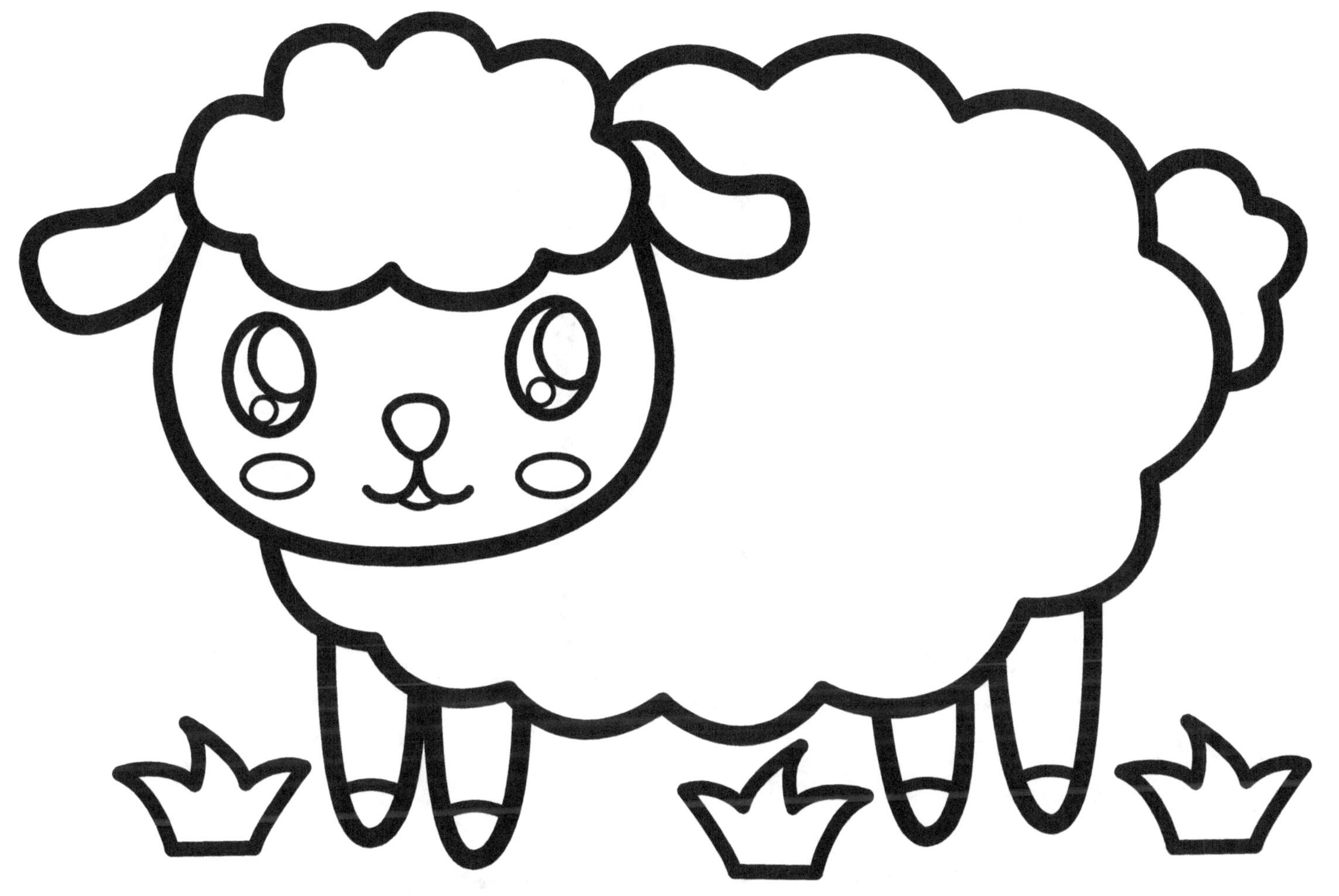

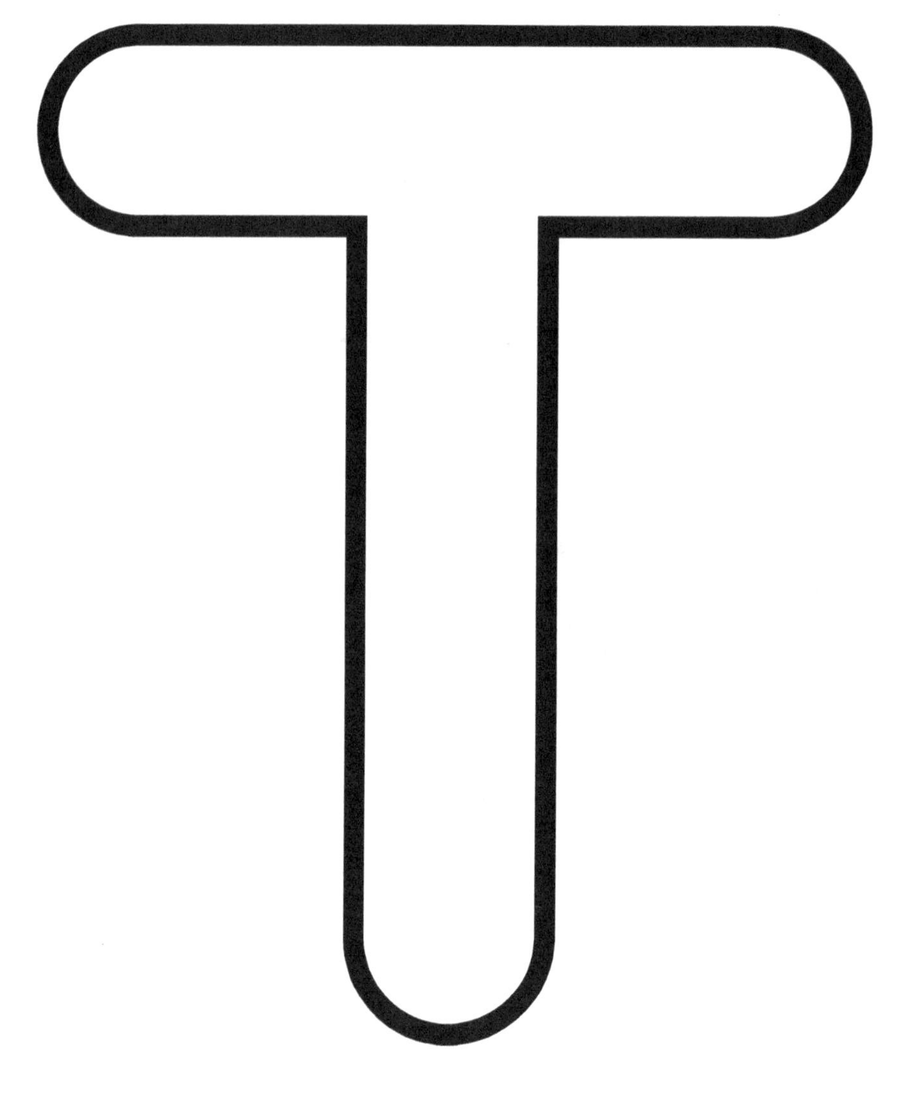

TIGER

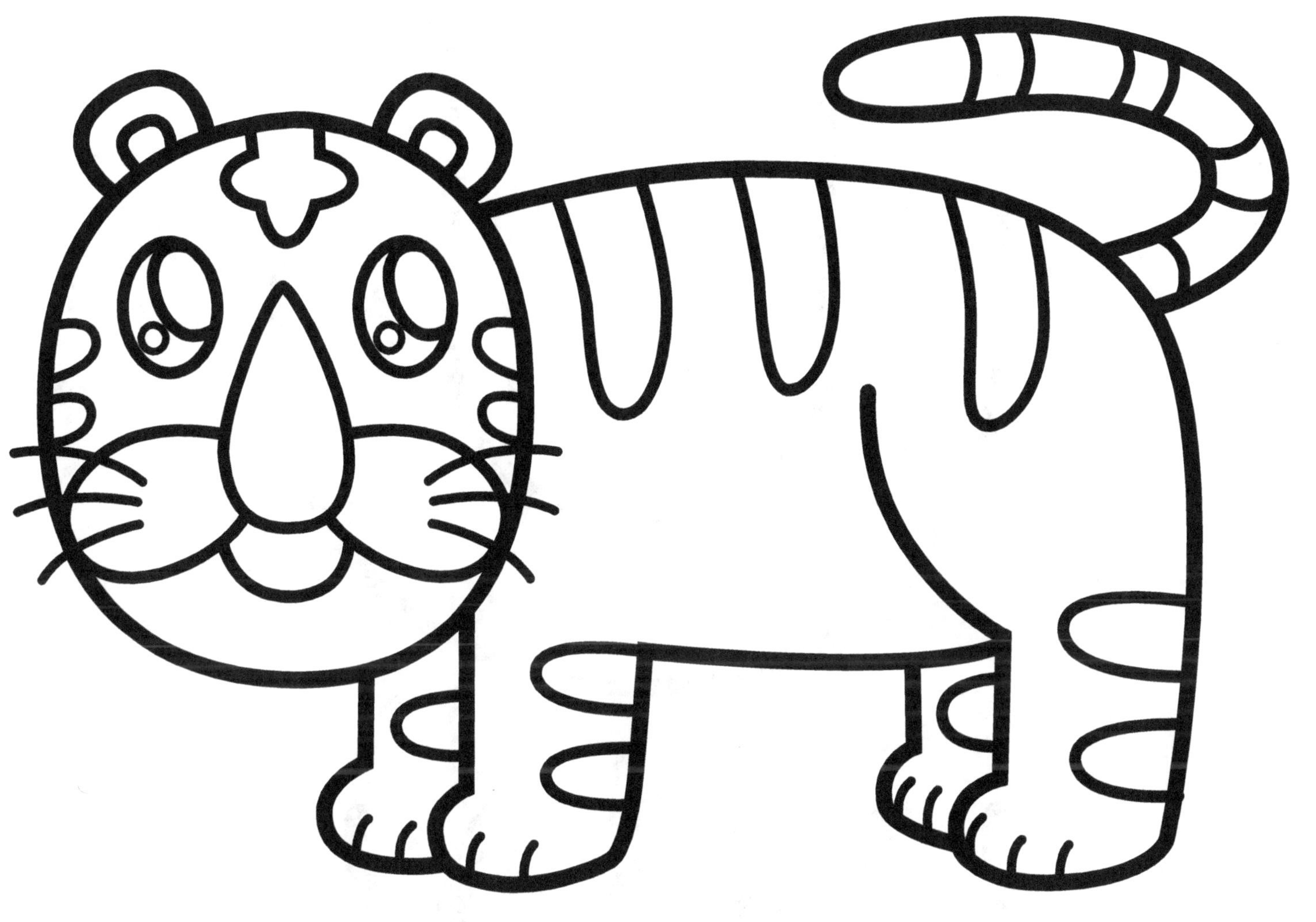

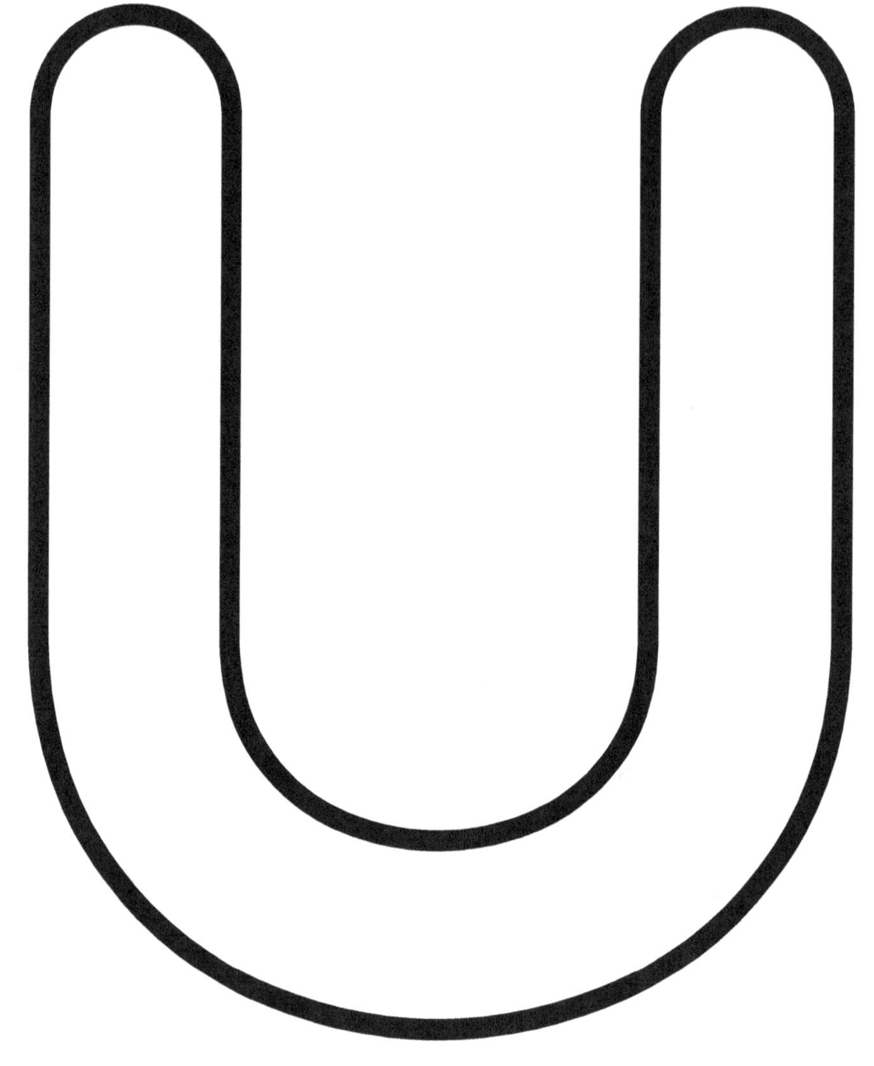


URIAL

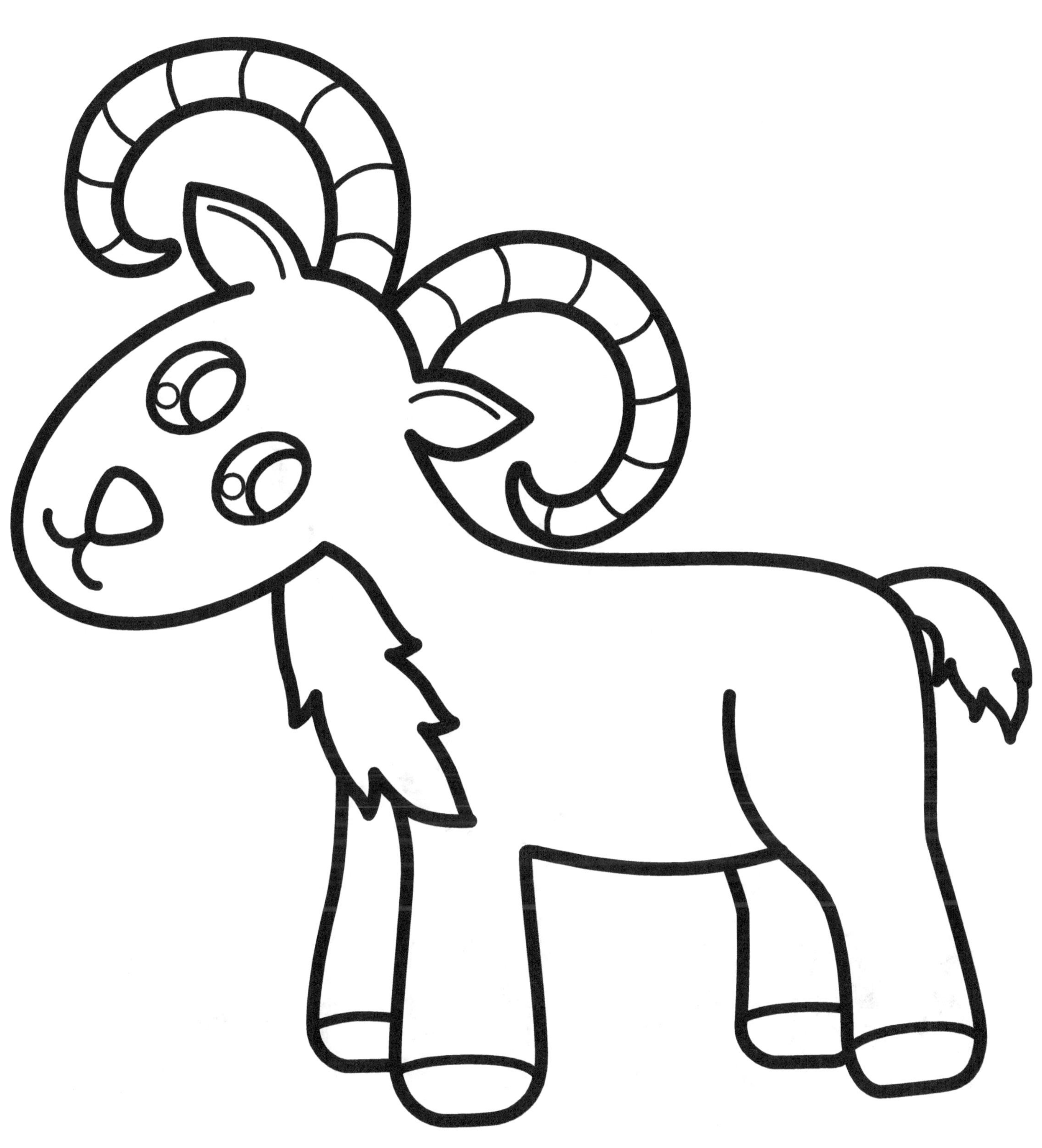

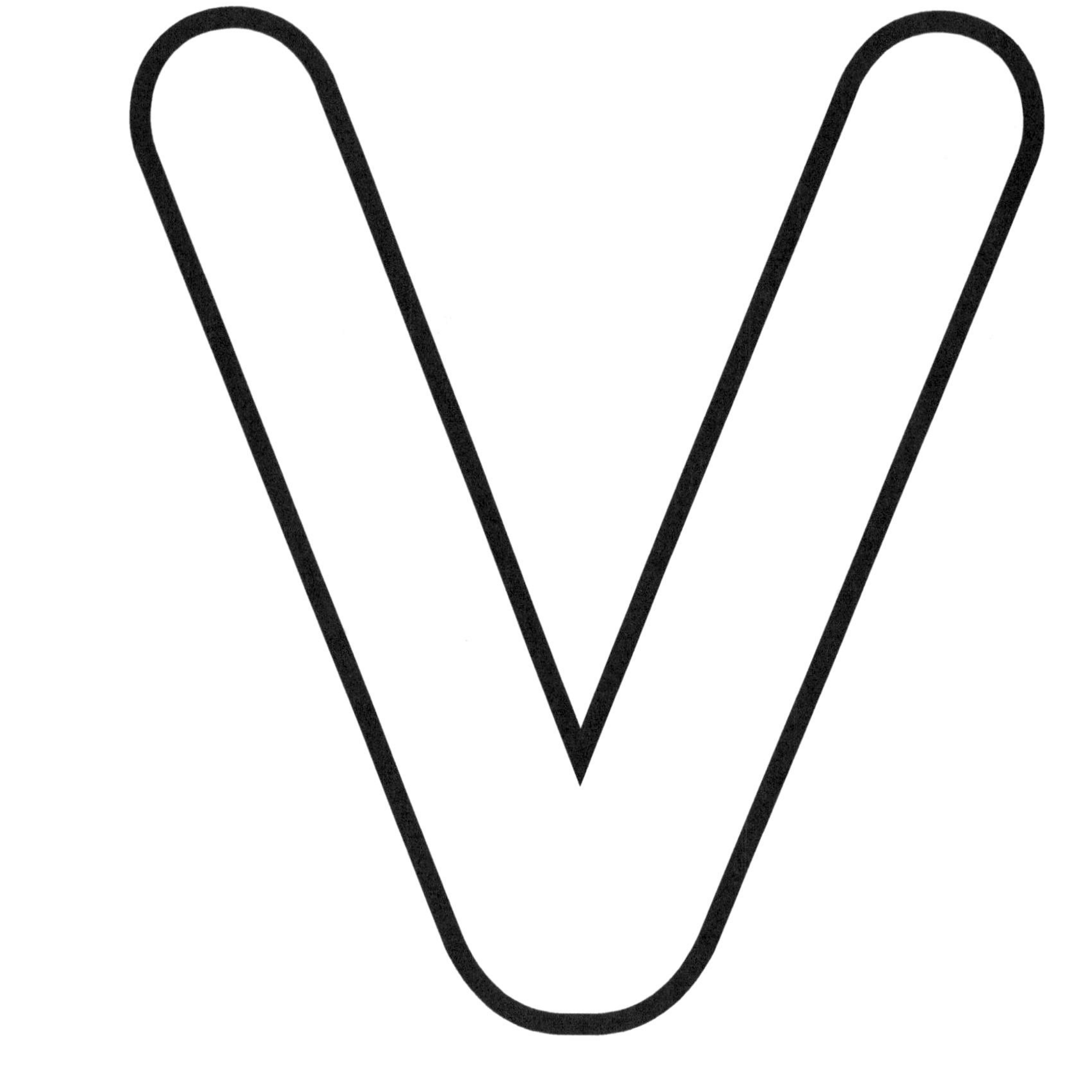

VULTURE

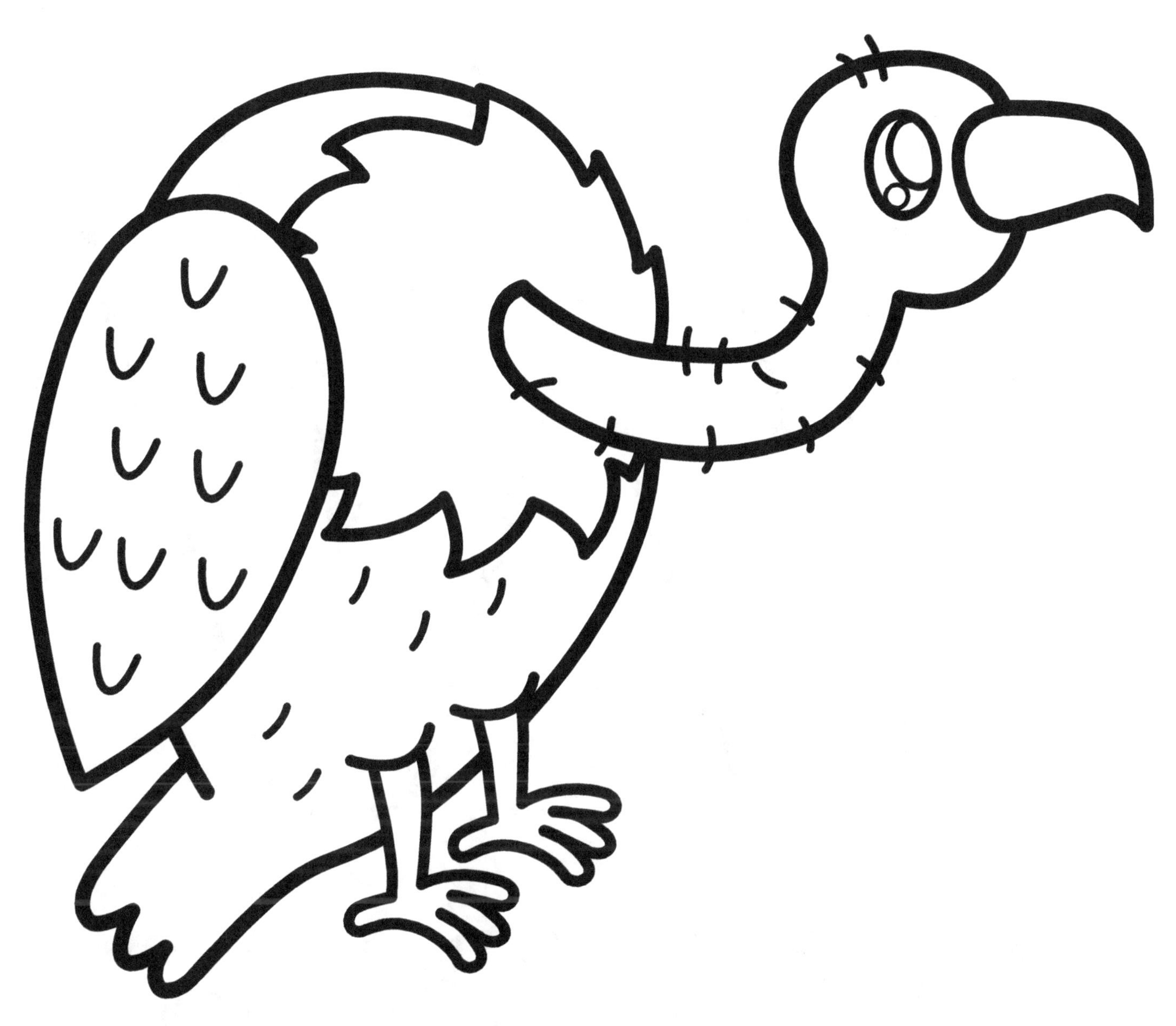

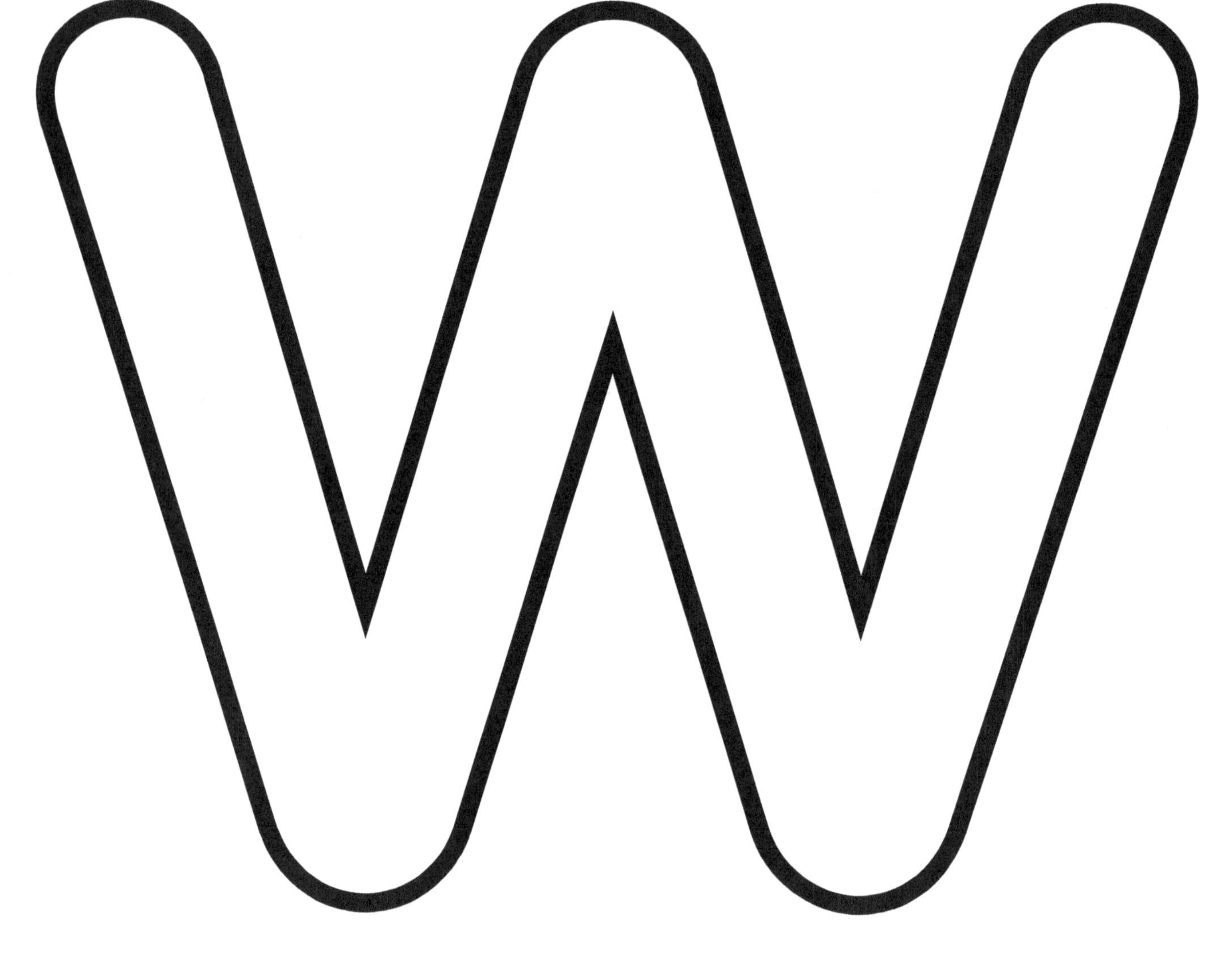

WALRUS

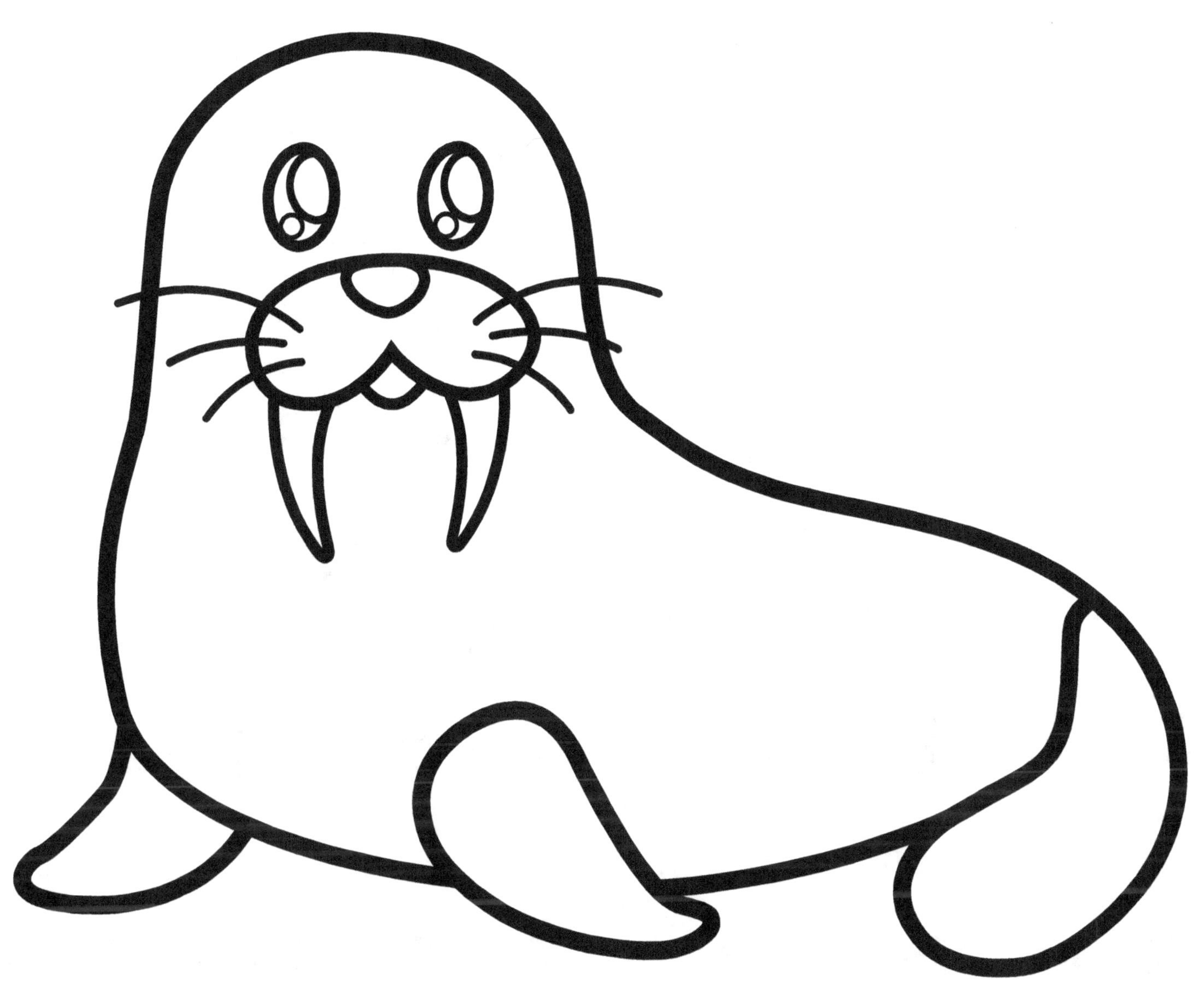

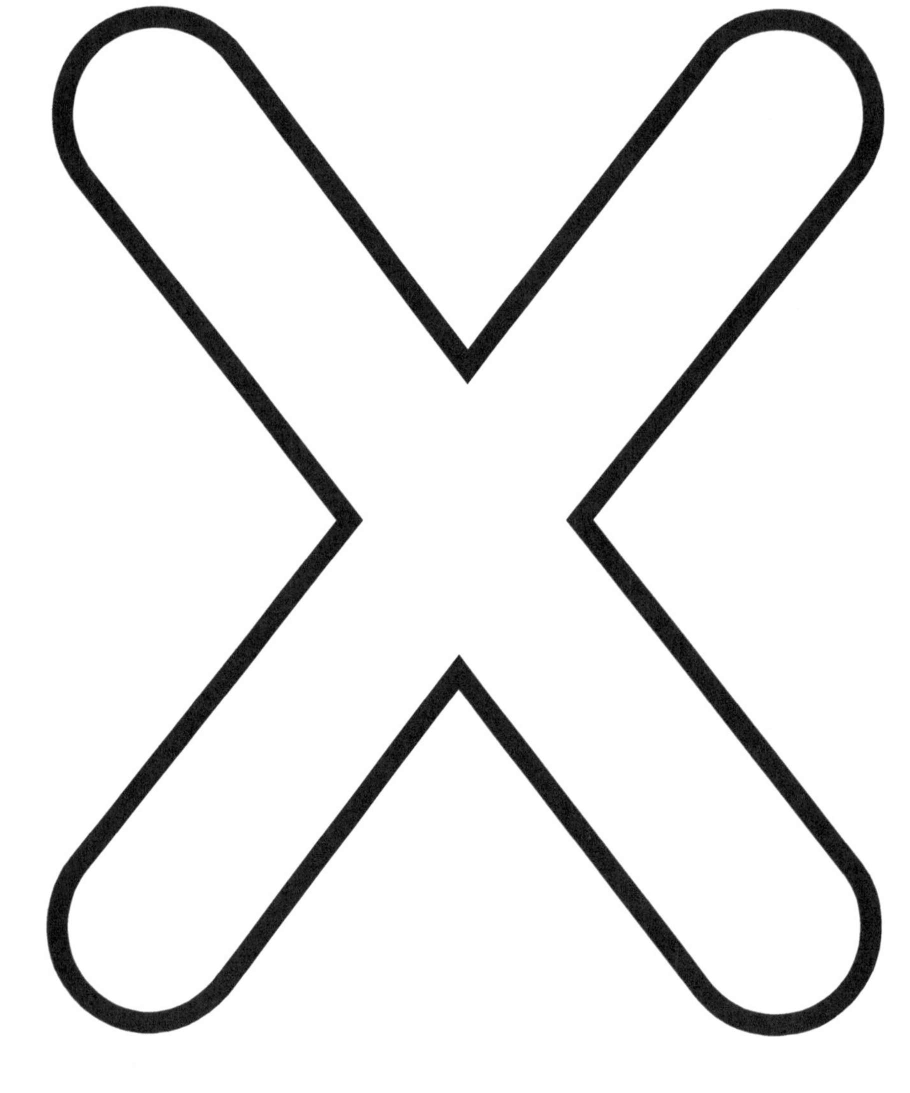
X-RAY FISH

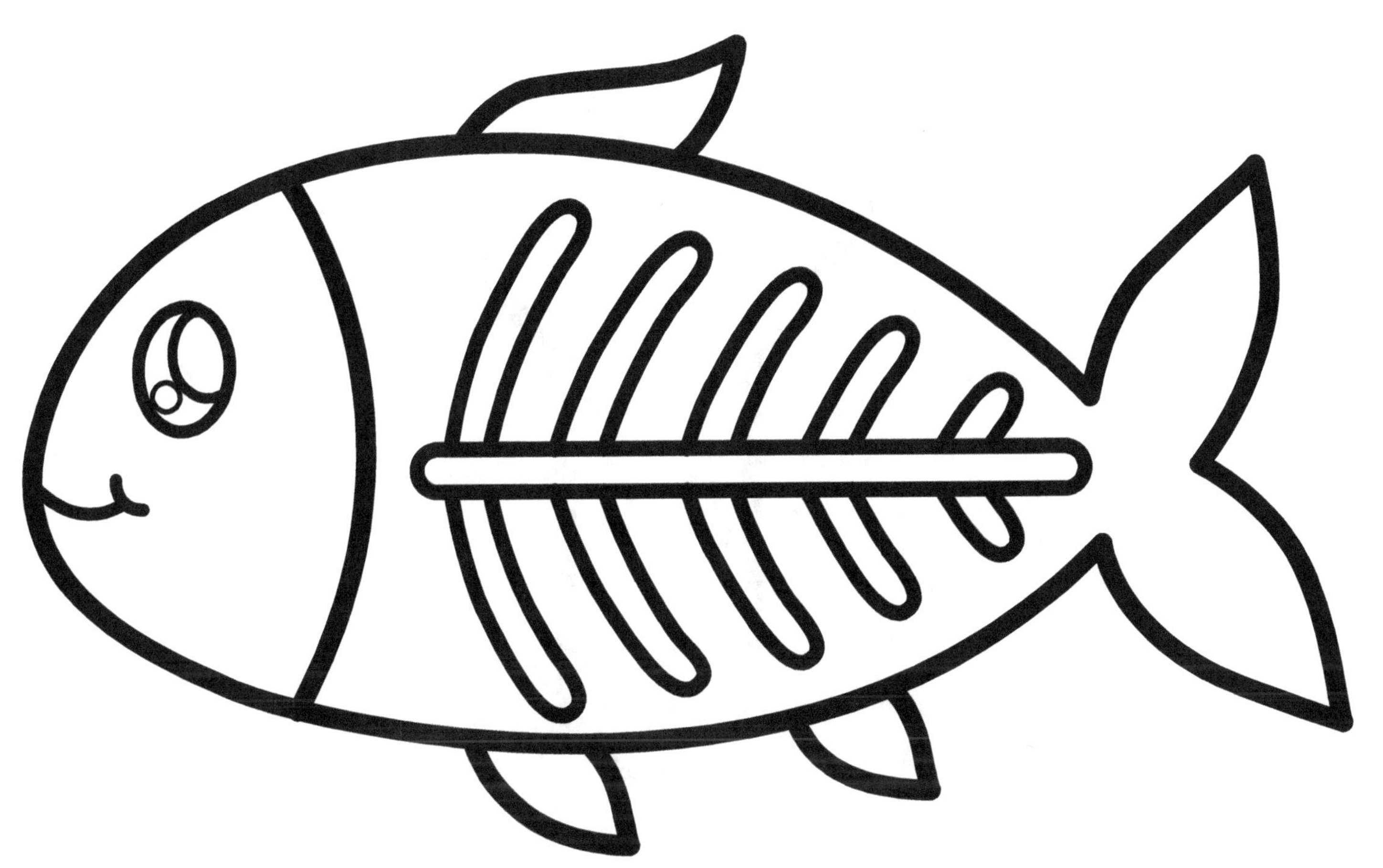

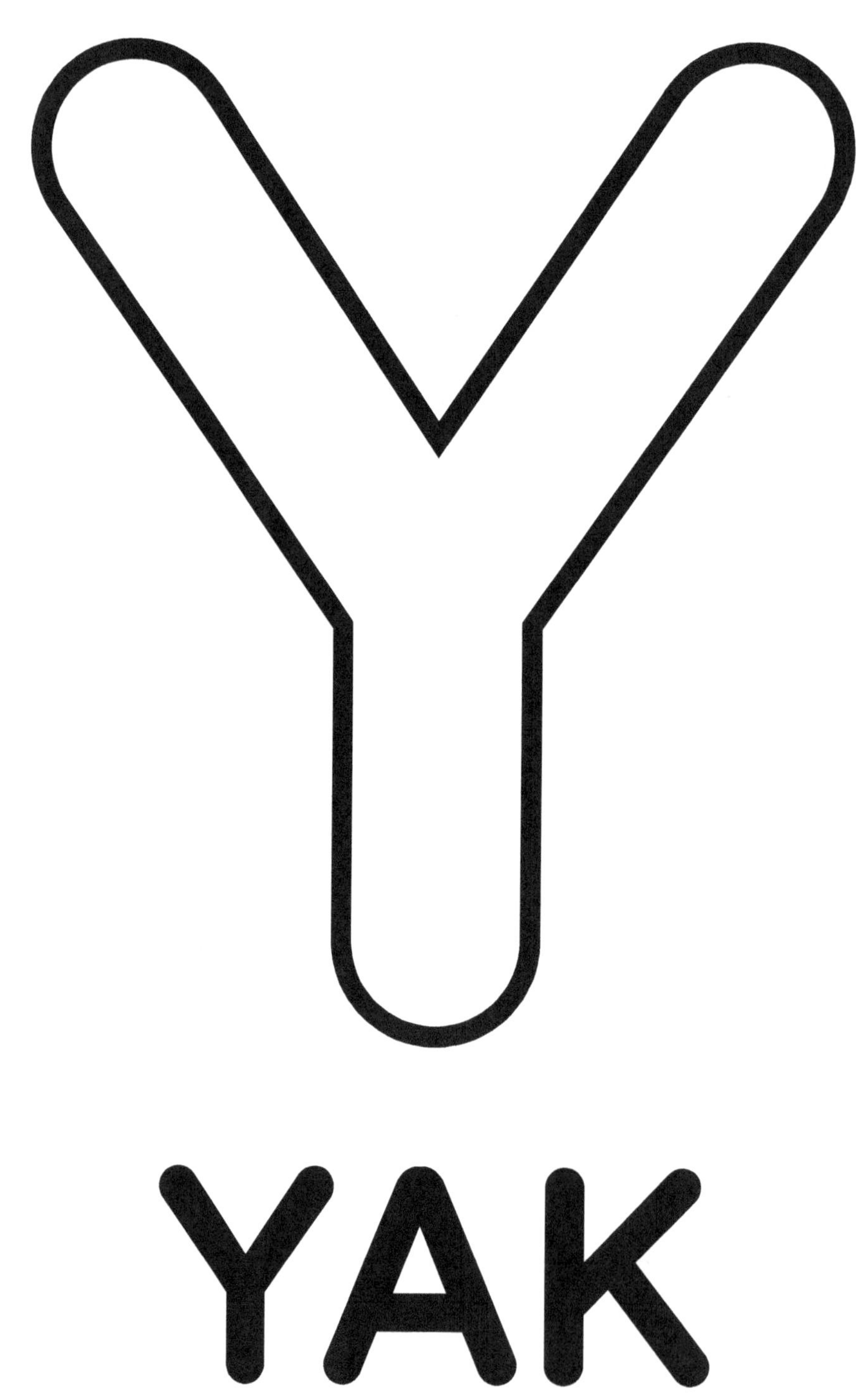

YAK

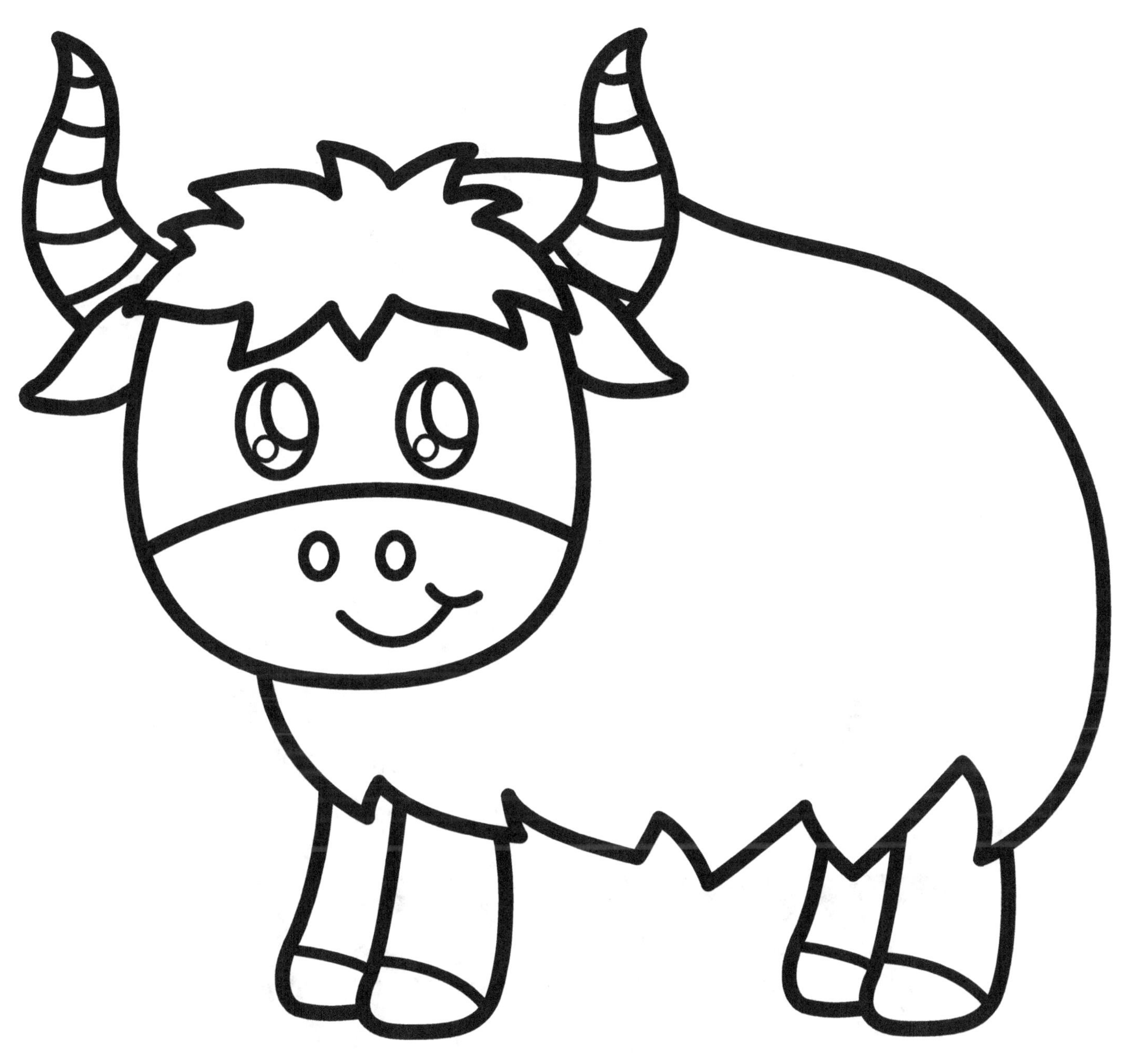

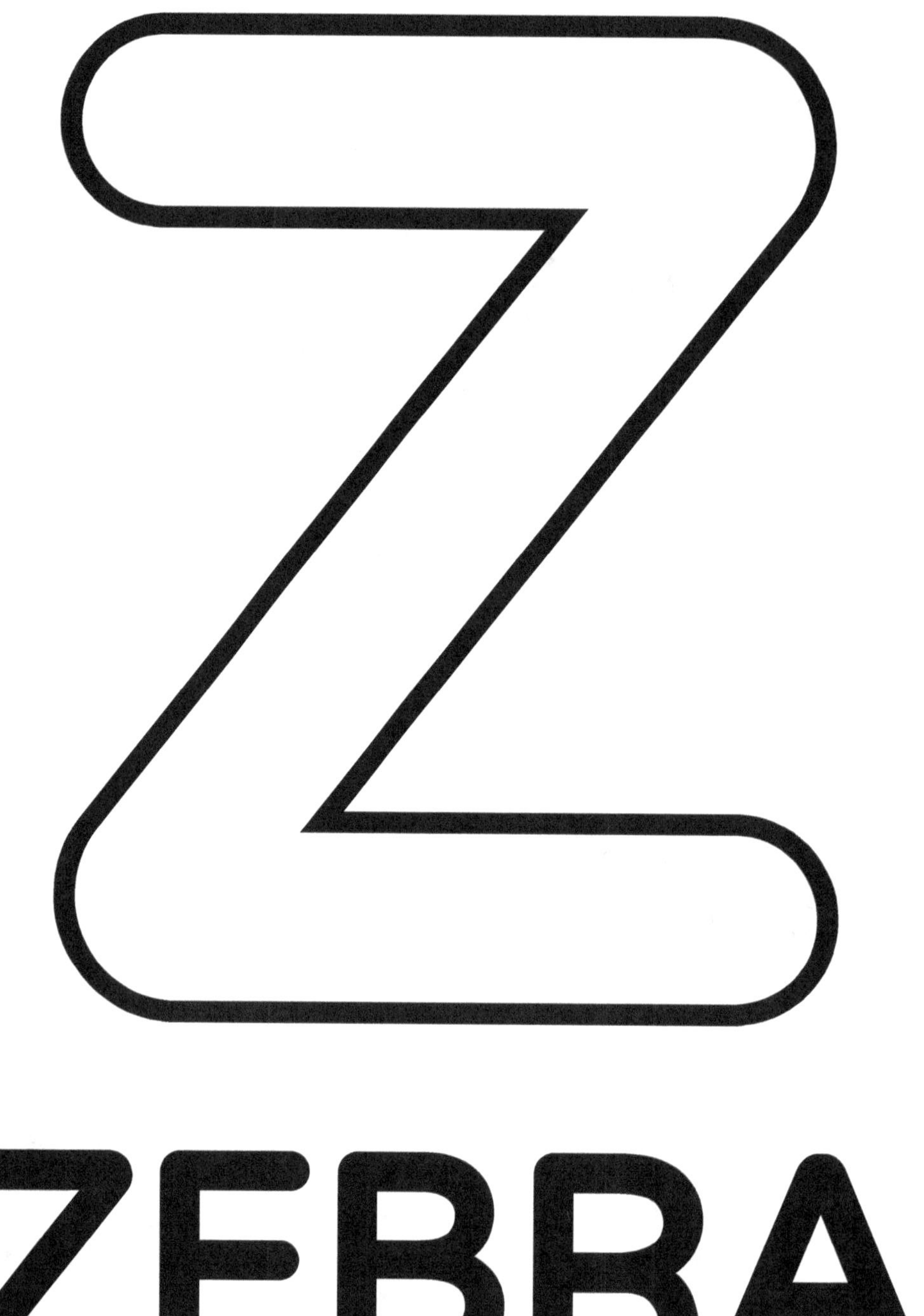

ZEBRA

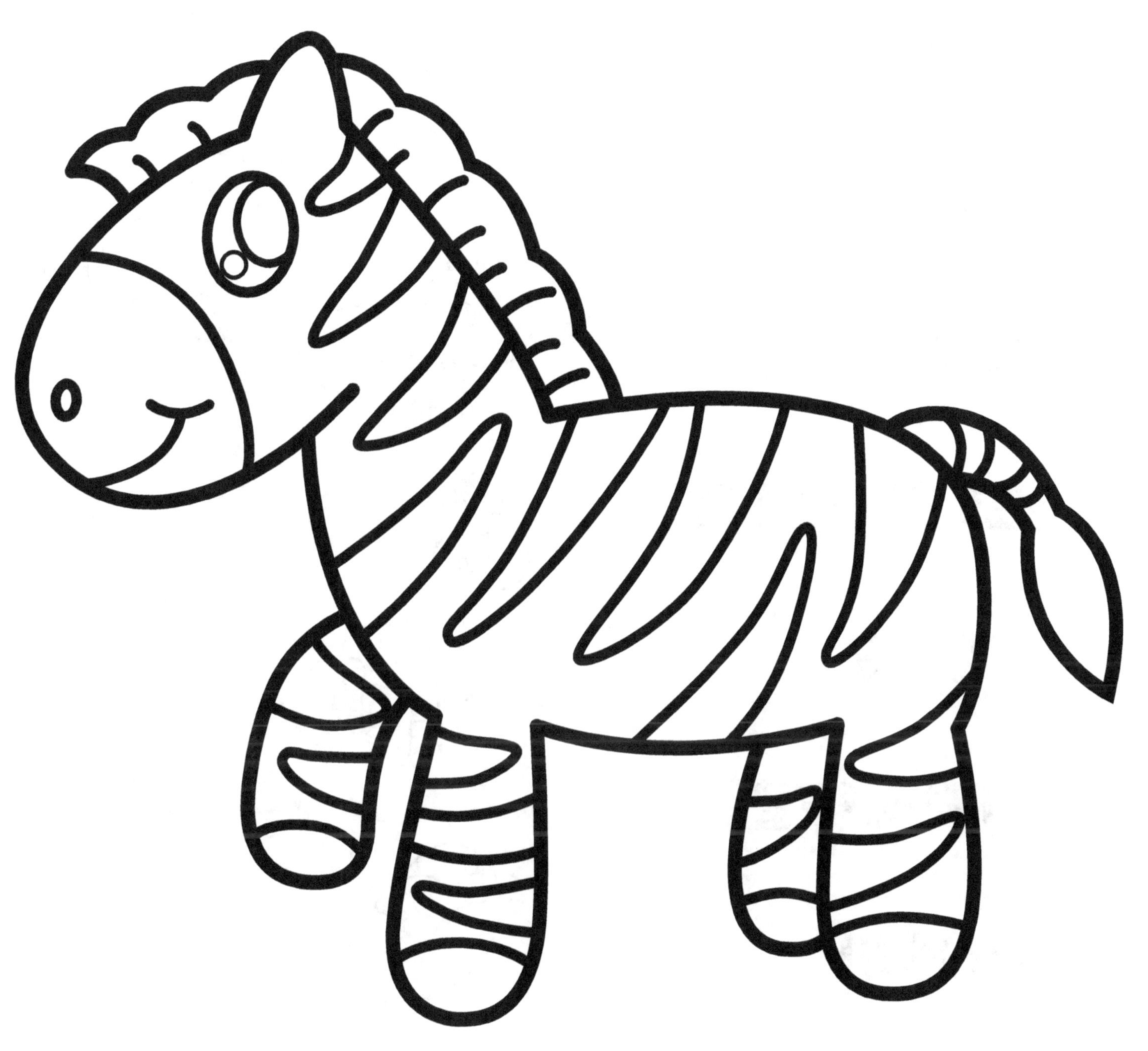

**ANT**

**BIRD**

**CAT**

**DUCK**

**ELEPHANT**

**FROG**

**GIRAFFE**

**HORSE**

**IGUANA**

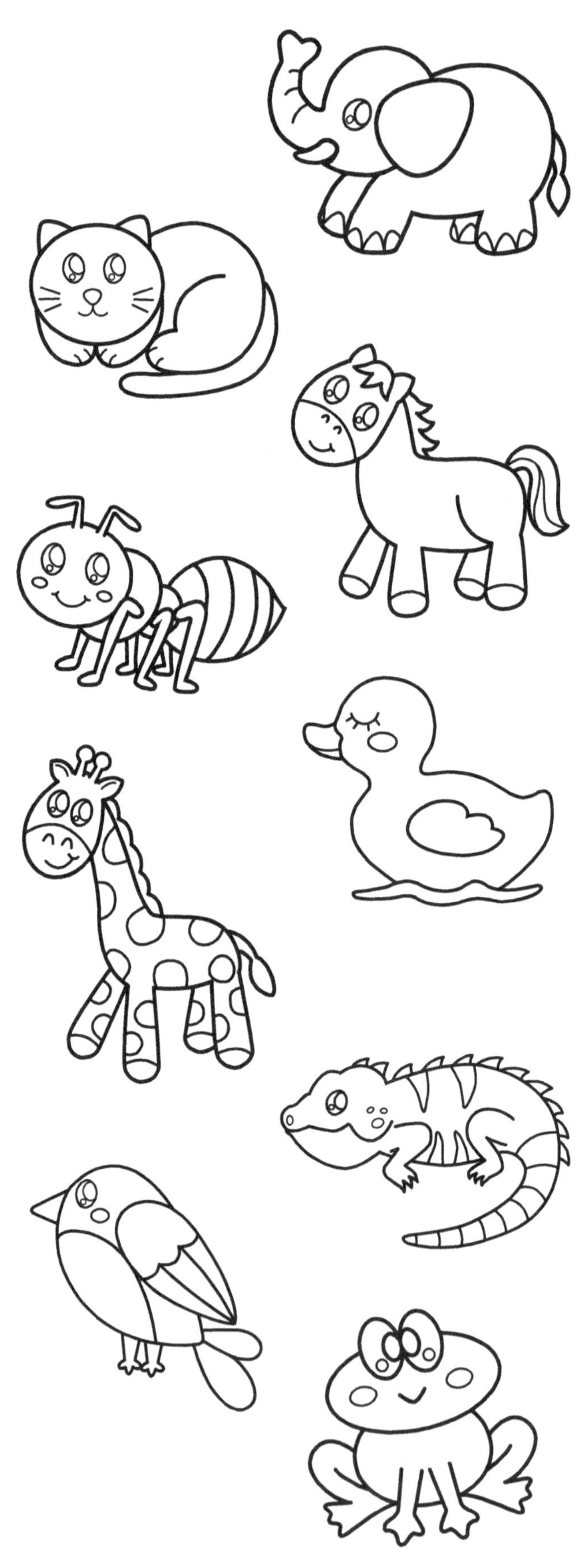

JELLY FISH

KOALA

LION

MONKEY

NAR WHAL

OWL

PIG

QUIL

RABBIT

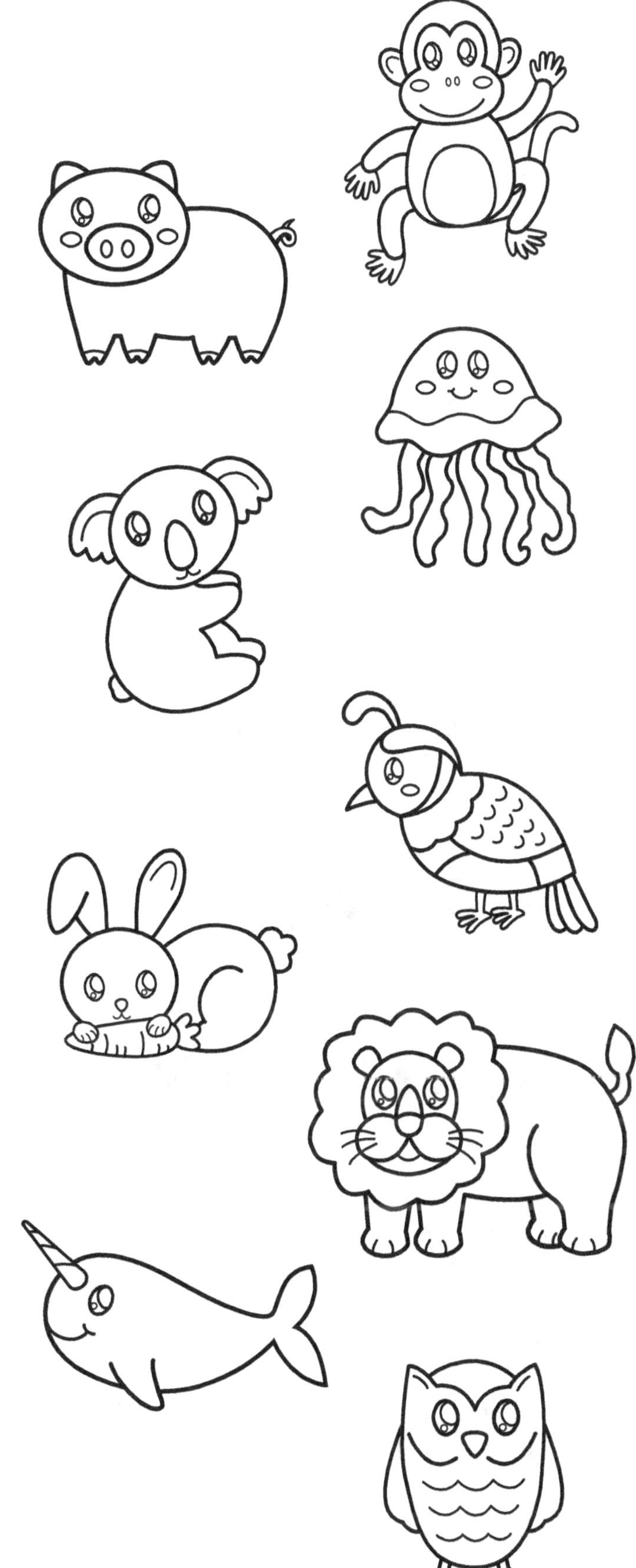

SHEEP

TIGER

URIAL

VULTURE

WALRUS

X-RAY FISH

YAK

ZEBRA

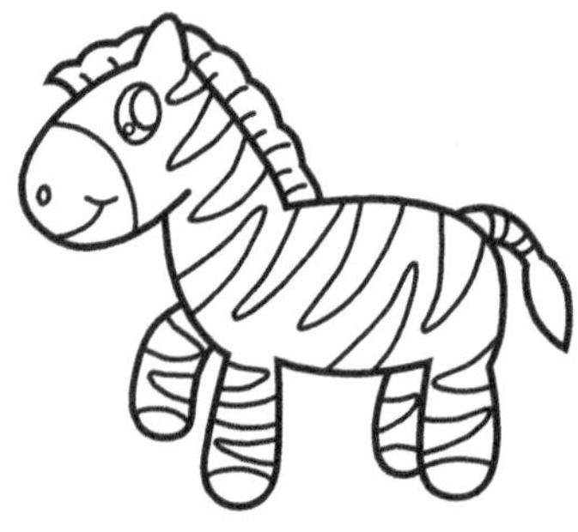

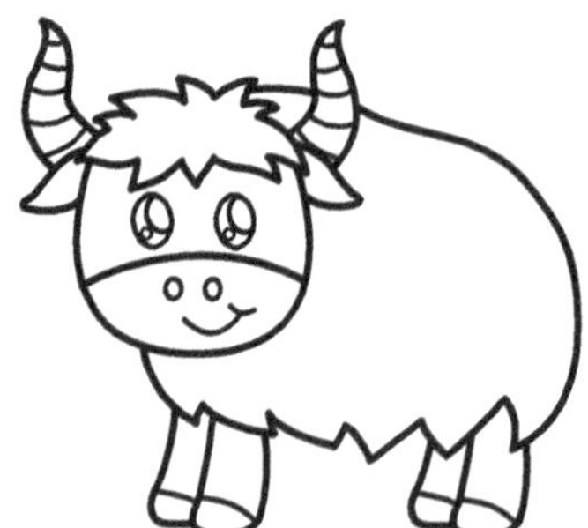

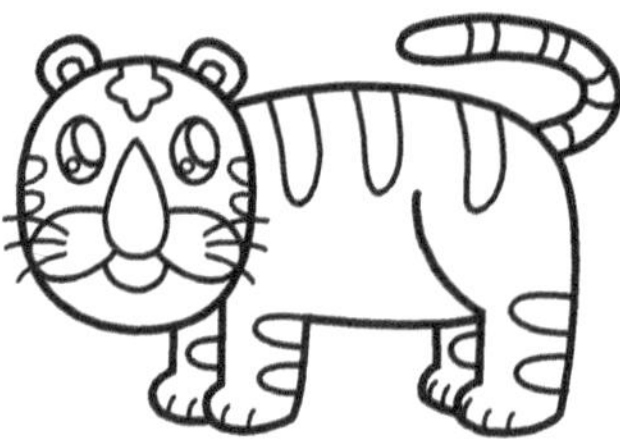

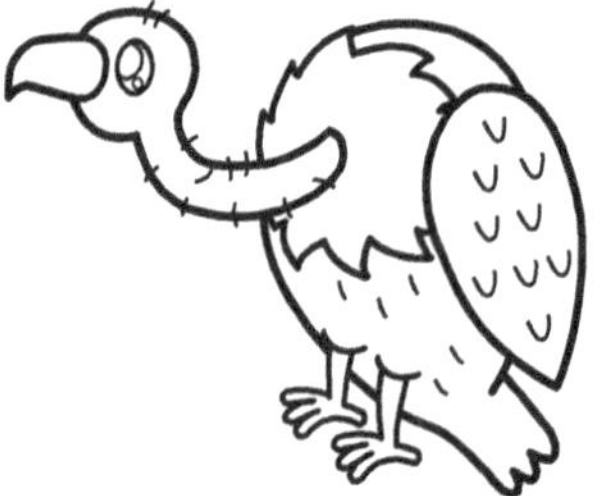

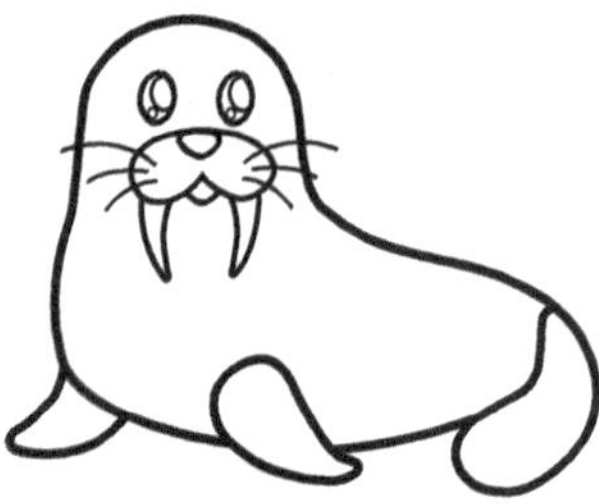

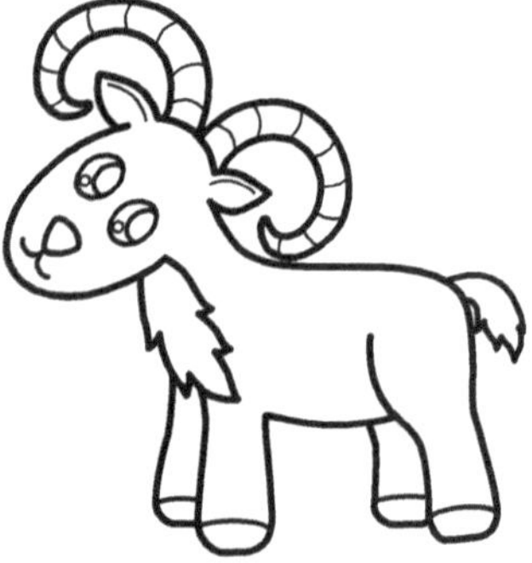

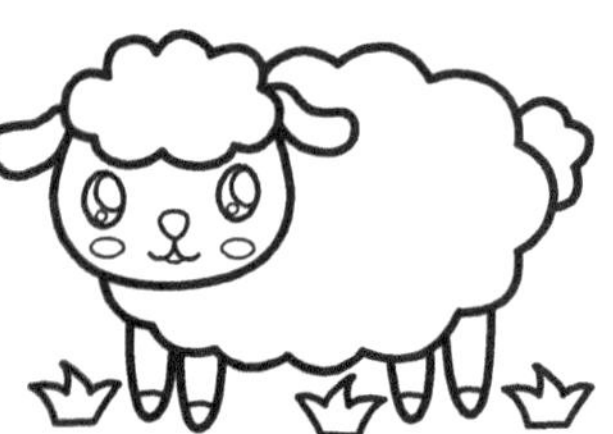

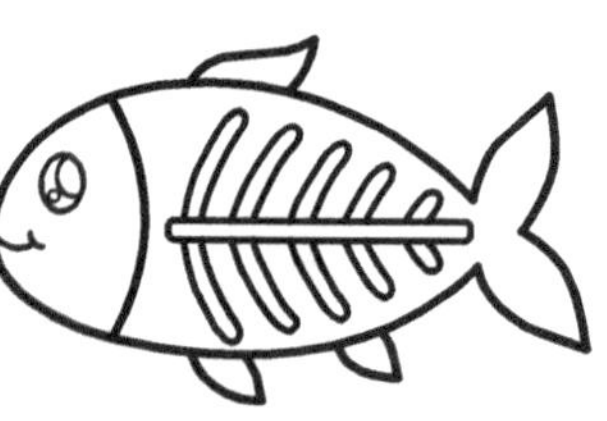